WORLD HISTORY SERIES

HISTORY SERIES

The Reagan Years

Titles in the World History Series

WORLD
HISTORY SERIES

The Reagan Years

by
Darv Johnson

Lucent Books, P.O. Box 289011, San Diego, CA 92198-9011

Library of Congress Cataloging-in-Publication Data

Johnson, Darv. 1971–
    The Reagan years / by Darv Johnson.
        p.   cm.—(World history series)
    Includes bibliographical references and index.
    Summary: Discusses the years of Ronald Reagan's presidency, including his past political experience, the Star Wars arms program, second term election, Iran-Contra scandal, and Reaganomics.
    ISBN 1-56006-592-3 (lib. : alk. paper)
    1. Reagan, Ronald—Juvenile literature. 2. Presidents—United States Biography—Juvenile literature. 3. Governors—California—Biography—Juvenile literature. 4. Motion picture actors and actresses—United States Biography Juvenile literature. 5. United States—Politics and government—1981–1989 Juvenile literature. [1. Reagan, Ronald. 2. Presidents. 3. United States—Politics and government—1981–1989.] I. Title. II. Series.
E877.J64   2000
973.927'092—dc21   99-35592
[B]   CIP

Copyright 2000 by Lucent Books, Inc., P.O. Box 289011, San Diego, California 92198-9011

Printed in the U.S.A.

Contents

Foreword

Each year on the first day of school, nearly every history teacher faces the task of explaining why his or her students should study history. One logical answer to this question is that exploring what happened in our past explains how the things we often take for granted—our customs, ideas, and institutions—came to be. As statesman and historian Winston Churchill put it, "Every nation or group of nations has its own tale to tell. Knowledge of the trials and struggles is necessary to all who would comprehend the problems, perils, challenges, and opportunities which confront us today." Thus, a study of history puts modern ideas and institutions in perspective. For example, though the founders of the United States were talented and creative thinkers, they clearly did not invent the concept of democracy. Instead, they adapted some democratic ideas that had originated in ancient Greece and with which the Romans, the British, and others had experimented. An exploration of these cultures, then, reveals their very real connection to us through institutions that continue to shape our daily lives.

Another reason often given for studying history is the idea that lessons exist in the past from which contemporary societies can benefit and learn. This idea, although controversial, has always been an intriguing one for historians. Those who agree that society can benefit from the past often quote philosopher George Santayana's famous statement, "Those who cannot remember the past are condemned to repeat it." Historians who subscribe to Santayana's philosophy believe that, for example, studying the events that led up to the major world wars or other significant historical events would allow society to chart a different and more favorable course in the future.

Just as difficult as convincing students to realize the importance of studying history is the search for useful and interesting supplementary materials that present historical events in a context that can be easily understood. The volumes in Lucent Books' World History Series attempt to present a broad, balanced, and penetrating view of the march of history. Ancient Egypt's important wars and rulers, for example, are presented against the rich and colorful backdrop of Egyptian religious, social, and cultural developments. The series engages the reader by enhancing historical events with these cultural contexts. For example, in *Ancient Greece,* the text covers the role of women in that society. Slavery is discussed in *The Roman Empire,* as well as how slaves earned their freedom. The numerous and varied aspects of every-day life in these and other societies are explored in each volume of the series. Additionally, the series covers the major political, cultural, and philosophical ideas as the torch of civilization is passed from ancient Mesopotamia and Egypt, through Greece, Rome, Medieval Europe, and other world cultures, to the modern day.

The material in the series is formatted in a thorough, precise, and organized manner. Each volume offers the reader a comprehensive and clearly written overview of an important historical event or period. The topic under discussion is placed in a broad, historical context. For example, The Italian Renaissance begins with a discussion of the High Middle Ages and the loss of central control that allowed certain Italian cities to develop artistically. The book ends by looking forward to the Reformation and interpreting the societal changes that grew out of the Renaissance. Thus, students are not only involved in an historical era, but also enveloped by the events leading up to that era and the events following it.

One important and unique feature in the World History Series is the primary and secondary source quotations that richly supplement each volume. These quotes are useful in a number of ways. First, they allow students access to sources they would not normally be exposed to because of the difficulty and obscurity of the original source. The quotations range from interesting anecdotes to far-sighted cultural perspectives and are drawn from historical witnesses both past and present. Second, the quotes demonstrate how and where historians themselves derive their information on the past as they strive to reach a consensus on historical events. Lastly, all of the quotes are footnoted, familiarizing students with the citation process and allowing them to verify quotes and/or look up the original source if the quote piques their interest.

Finally, the books in the World History Series provide a detailed launching point for further research. Each book contains a bibliography specifically geared toward student research. A second, annotated bibliography introduces students to all the sources the author consulted when compiling the book. A chronology of important dates gives students an overview, at a glance, of the topic covered. Where applicable, a glossary of terms is included.

In short, the series is designed not only to acquaint readers with the basics of history, but also to make them aware that their lives are a part of an ongoing human saga. Perhaps they will then come to the same realization as famed historian Arnold Toynbee. In his monumental work, A Study of History, he wrote about becoming aware of history flowing through him in a mighty current, and of his own life "welling like a wave in the flow of this vast tide."

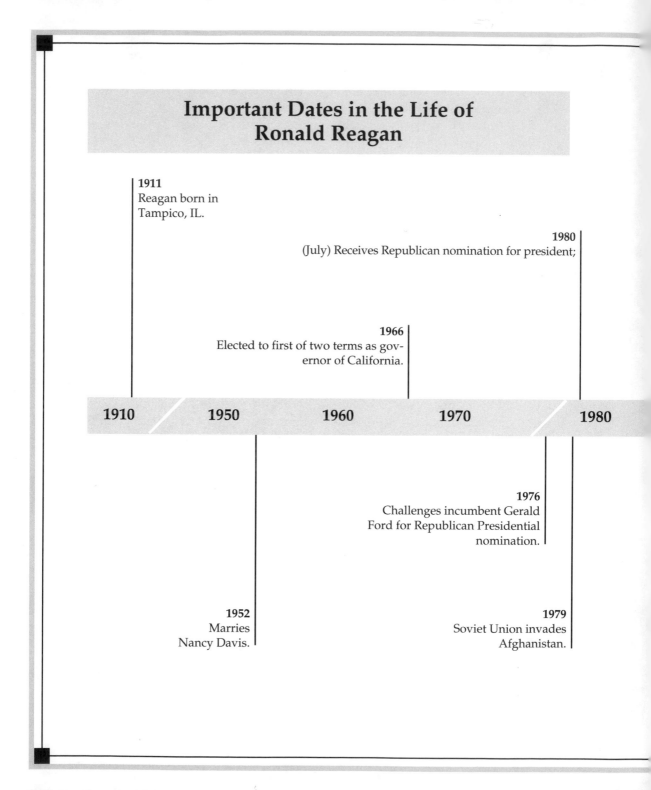

Important Dates in the Life of Ronald Reagan

1911
Reagan born in Tampico, IL.

1980
(July) Receives Republican nomination for president;

1966
Elected to first of two terms as governor of California.

| 1910 | 1950 | 1960 | 1970 | 1980 |

1976
Challenges incumbent Gerald Ford for Republican Presidential nomination.

1952
Marries Nancy Davis.

1979
Soviet Union invades Afghanistan.

1983
(September) Soviet Union shoots down Korean airliner, straining relations with United States; (October) U.S. forces invade West Indies island of Grenada to rid it of Marxist government; terrorist attack at U.S. Embassy in Beirut, Lebanon kills 241 American servicemen.

1982
Annual federal budget deficit surpasses $100 billion for first time in history.

1984
(October) Boland II Amendment is signed, outlawing CIA support of the contras; (November) Reagan defeats Walter Mondale to win second term.

1986
(January) Space shuttle *Challenger* explodes, killing seven American astronauts; (April) U.S. jets bomb Libya in retaliation for its terrorist actions; (October) Second round of arms negotiations with Gorbachev held in Iceland; (November) First reports of Iran-contra affair appear in the news.

1988–89
Soviet troops withdrawn from Afghanistan.

1982	1984	1986	1988	1990

1985
(January) Second term in office begins; (March) Mikhail Gorbachev becomes General Secretary of the Communist party; (August) Reagan agrees to secretly sell arms to Iran in return for release of American prisoners; (November) Reagan and Soviet leader Mikhail Gorbachev open arms control talks in Geneva.

1989
(January) After inauguration of successor George Bush, Reagan retires to California; (November) Berlin Wall falls, signifying the end of the Cold War.

1981
(January) Begins first term in office; fifty-two U.S. hostages held in Iran are released; (March) Reagan authorizes $20 million in aid to the Nicaraguan contras; John Hinckley wounds Reagan and three of his staff with six shots from a revolver; (July) Reagan nominates Sandra Day O'Connor to be first female member of the Supreme Court; (October) Egyptian president Anwar Sadat, supporter of peace in Middle East, is assassinated.

1987
(February) Tower Commission report criticizes Reagan for his part in Iran-contra scandal; (May) Reagan makes first speech on the subject of AIDS; (October) Stock market crashes; (December) Gorbachev and Reagan sign INF Treaty to limit medium- and short-range missiles.

Reagan Takes the Stage

The events of the 1960s and 1970s—war in Vietnam, troubled presidencies, economic stumbles—shook the United States. The American people, said President Jimmy Carter in 1979, were left suffering from "a crisis of confidence . . . that strikes at the very heart and soul and spirit of our national will."[1] Seeking assurances that the future would be brighter, in 1980 the country poured its hopes and dreams into an actor-turned-politician, Ronald Wilson Reagan.

Reagan had made the long journey from Depression-era poverty to movie star, millionaire, and governor of the nation's most populous state. He clung to his small-town beliefs in God, country, and the value of hard work while succeeding at the highest levels of politics. America gave Reagan opportunities, and he made the most of them.

Reagan had always played the good guy in Hollywood movies, and it was this

Ronald Reagan was elected president in 1980. Many people believed that he brought hope to the country at a time when it was still recovering from past troubles.

heroic role that many Americans wanted him to fill again when they elected him president in 1980. With his reassuring words and calming presence, he inspired millions to believe in him and his vision of America. "The truth is there are simple answers—there are not always easy ones," he declared on many occasions.[2] His simple and unshakable belief was that lower taxes, less government interference, and a strong military could cure America. His message was positive, and it carried the conviction that America was the greatest nation on earth.

At the beginning of his presidency, Reagan used the power of his popularity to drive his conservative economic and foreign policies through Congress. His admirers hoped that his early success was the beginning of a radical change in the direction of American politics, a "Reagan Revolution" that they hoped would restore the moral, religious, patriotic, and conservative values that they felt had been missing from the national government for half a century.

Reagan was so charismatic that his seeming contradictions were often over-looked: Reagan, the leader of the conservative party, was once an outspoken liberal; he warned against excessive government spending while allowing the federal budget to grow larger than ever before; he projected the image of a strong, decisive leader, yet insiders described him as disengaged; he preached a hard line against terrorists, while secretly selling them weapons; he was fiercely anticommunist but was willing to negotiate with the leader of the Communist bloc, Soviet president Mikhail Gorbachev, to end the nuclear arms race.

Reagan, however, was untroubled by these gaps between words and deeds. When he made his last address to the nation on January 11, 1989, there was no doubt in his mind that his leadership had worked for America:

> [A]s long as we remember our first principles and believe in ourselves, the future will always be ours. And something else we learned: Once you begin a great movement, there is no telling where it will end. We meant to change a nation, and instead, we changed a world.[3]

1 The Road to the White House

In 1980, as Ronald Reagan traveled around the country in his campaign for the presidency of the United States, he repeatedly asked voters a simple question: "Just ask yourself, are you better off now than you were four years ago?"[4]

For the majority of Americans, the answer to this question was a resounding "no." Economically and emotionally, the nation had reached the low point of a decline that began with the assassination of President John F. Kennedy in 1963. The seventeen years in between were marred by a series of unsettling events: a costly war in Vietnam; urban riots; the assassinations of presidential candidate Robert Kennedy and civil rights leaders Martin Luther King Jr. and Malcolm X; an accelerating nuclear arms race with the Soviet Union; an energy crisis; and a long period of economic hardship.

The stature and dignity of the office of president had suffered along with the nation. Following President Kennedy's death, Lyndon B. Johnson's handling of the war in Vietnam led to unprecedented questioning of the president's judgment. In the face of fierce resistance in America to the war and mounting U.S. casualties in Southeast Asia, Johnson declined to seek reelection and left office in January 9, 1969.

The newly elected president, Richard Nixon, promised to lead the country out of the Vietnam War. The withdrawal was not as quick as many Americans desired, however. The eruption of the Watergate scandal in the spring of 1973 put an end to Nixon's presidency. Nixon and members of his reelection committee were accused of spying on their opponents and accepting corporate contributions in return for political favors. The scandal forced Nixon to resign from office in August 1974.

When Nixon left office in disgrace, his vice president, Gerald Ford, became president. Ford's term was marked by an inability to prop up a faltering national economy. Meanwhile, his decision to grant Nixon a full pardon for his role in the Watergate scandal attracted a storm of public criticism and contributed to his loss to Jimmy Carter in the 1976 presidential election.

Carter pledged that he would never lie to the American people, a promise that would have perhaps been taken for granted in the pre-Nixon days. While many Americans greeted his informal management style in the White House as a

President Richard Nixon's role in the Watergate scandal outraged the public and resulted in his resignation from office.

welcome break from the aloof presidency of Nixon, he was criticized for appearing tentative and indecisive on political issues. Carter failed to pass major legislation through Congress, contributing to a sense that the president was powerless to lead the country. Meanwhile, an energy crisis triggered by a trade dispute with the major oil-producing nations caused long lines at the gasoline pumps. Traditionally strong industries, such as steel, automobile, and construction, suffered in the worsening economic conditions. The combined rates

of inflation—the rise in the cost of living—and unemployment reached a record 19 percent in 1980, nearly four percentage points higher than they were when Carter took office.

Internationally, the United States was faring just as poorly. A 1979 revolution in Iran ousted the American-backed Iranian leader Shah Muhammad Reza Pahlavi, and replaced him with the Ayatollah Khomeini, who was hostile to the United States. The situation soon became a crisis when a mob in the Iranian capital of Tehran stormed the U.S. Embassy and took fifty-two Americans hostage, demanding the return of the shah, who had fled to the United States. Carter worked tirelessly to gain the safe release of the hostages, but his attempts—including an ill-fated military rescue mission that resulted in the deaths of American soldiers—failed. The crisis left the impression that the United States was at the mercy of a much smaller country. Many Americans were humiliated by this blow to the nation's prestige.

To make matters worse, the Soviet Union loomed ever larger as a threat to world peace. In December 1979, the Soviets invaded the central Asian country of Afghanistan, sparking fears that the country would fall under Communist rule. At the same time, the Soviets continued to add to their arsenal of nuclear weapons. Despite negotiations between Carter and Soviet leaders, no meaningful progress was made to improve U.S.-Soviet relations, which had been hostile since the end of World War II because of ideological and political differences.

WHERE HE CAME FROM

When Ronald Reagan was nominated as the Republican candidate for president in the spring of 1980, he stepped into the middle of this unsettled economic and political climate. Drawing heavily on his past experiences and life story, he tried to convince voters that he could put America back on course.

From the beginning, Reagan was immersed in the values and traditions of small-town America: patriotism, strong family bonds, and hard work. He was born in 1911 in Tampico, Illinois, and spent most of his childhood in Dixon, another small town nearby. His summers revolved around playing with fireworks and swimming in the Rock River. As a fourteen-year-old, he got his first job working construction for thirty-five cents an hour. Later he became the lifeguard in a local park, drum major, class president, and a starter on his high school football team.

Reagan's father was an alcoholic, and the family's economic fortunes suffered as a result. They lived in small, rented houses, owned no luxury items, and occasionally went without gifts at Christmas. "Our family didn't exactly come from the wrong side of the tracks, but we were certainly always within sound of the train whistles," Reagan later wrote.[5] But in spite of the hardships, he remembers his early years fondly: "As I look back on

Reagan's middle-class upbringing made him appealing to the average voter. Here Reagan greets visitors at the opening of a library and museum named in his honor.

THE BUDDING CONSERVATIVE

In a 1951 speech to the Kiwanis International convention, reprinted in Reagan's Speaking My Mind, *Reagan discusses his fear of a communist takeover of the movie industry. He also complains about income taxes that he and other movie stars had to pay to the federal government.*

"We are pretty proud of the fact that our government says that in the ideological struggle that is going on on the screens of the world, it is the American motion picture, not with its message picture, just showing our store windows in the street scenes with the things that Americans can buy, our parking lots, our streets with the automobiles, that is holding back the flood of propaganda from the other side of the Iron Curtain. Last, but not least, we are most proud of the great tribute that was paid to us by the Kremlin in Moscow, when recently it said, 'The worst enemy of the [Russian] people, the worst tool of degenerate capitalism that must be destroyed is the motion picture screen of Hollywood, California.' We are proud of that tribute. . . .

You know that the Communists have tried to invade our industry and that we have fought them to the point where we now have them licked. But there are other more insidious and less obvious inroads being made at our democratic institutions by way of the motion picture industry. For example, no industry has been picked for such discriminatory taxes as have the individuals in the industry of motion pictures, and you don't realize that because the average citizen is too prone to say, 'They are all overpaid in Hollywood, so let it go at that,' but if they can get away with it there, it is aimed at your pocketbook and you are next."

those days in Dixon, I think my life was as sweet and idyllic as it could be, as close as I could imagine for a young boy to the world created by Mark Twain in *The Adventures of Tom Sawyer*."[6]

In the fall of 1928, Reagan enrolled at Eureka College, a small school not far from his hometown. While he was a mediocre student, Eureka exposed him to acting and public speaking, skills that he would rely on for the remainder of his working life. As a freshman, he led a student strike protesting the school president's plan to fire teachers in order to trim the school's expenses. The strike gave Reagan his first shot at public speaking, and he loved it.

It was also at Eureka that Reagan began acting in school plays, and discovered that he had some talent for it. After graduating, he talked his way into a job at a small radio station in Davenport, Iowa, and soon became a popular sports announcer. From there, it was a short leap to a career in Hollywood.

REAGAN GOES TO HOLLYWOOD

Following a screen test in 1937, Reagan was signed as an actor by Warner Brothers, a Hollywood studio. There he became a minor star, with roles in movies such as *King's Row, Bedtime for Bonzo,* and *Knute Rockne: All American*. His work on these and dozens of other motion pictures allowed him to polish his speaking skills and on-screen charm, qualities that would serve him well later as a political candidate.

Reagan's success in Hollywood also shaped his views on taxation. In the late 1940s, he signed a seven-year, $1 million contract with Warner Brothers. This salary placed him in the highest income tax bracket, which at the time meant that the federal government took about nine out of ten dollars he earned. Many other actors avoided this high tax by temporarily stopping work after making four films in a year, which dropped their income level. Decades later, Reagan still remembered how much he had disliked this heavy tax burden and how it cut into the productiv-

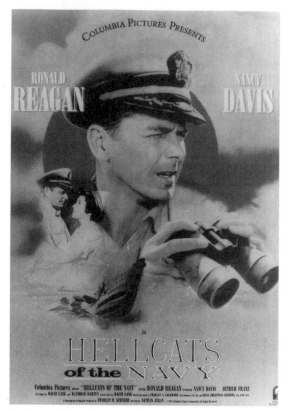

Reagan claims that the high taxes he paid while working as an actor marked the beginning of his dissatisfaction with big government.

ity of many of his fellow actors. He wrote in his 1990 autobiography:

> At the peak of my career at Warner Bros., I was in the ninety-four percent tax bracket; that meant that after a certain point, I received only six cents of each dollar I earned and the government got the rest. The IRS took such a big chunk of my earnings that after a while I began asking myself whether it was worth it to keep on taking work. Something was wrong with a system like that: When you have to give up such a large percent-

age of your income in taxes, incentive to work goes down.[7]

World War II broke out as Reagan neared the high point of his acting career. He stayed in California during the war, serving in the First Motion Picture Unit of the Army Air Corps and acting in pilot-training films.

The Soviet Union, the most powerful communist nation, was an ally of the United States in World War II. But when the war ended, many Americans grew suspicious that the Soviets were trying to force communist ideals on the American people. Led by a senator from Wisconsin named Joseph McCarthy, who gained prominence in the 1950s by leveling sensational and unsubstantiated charges of communism against U.S. officials, an anticommunist fervor swept the nation.

Reagan and others believed that Hollywood movies were the perfect vehicle for a communist plot. According to Reagan, [Soviet leader] "Joseph Stalin had set out to make Hollywood an instrument of propaganda for his program of Soviet expansionism aimed at communizing the world."[8] Reagan believed that Stalin's plan was to use Hollywood actors, writers, and producers who were sympathetic to the communist cause to inject procommunist themes into American movies.

Reagan threw himself into the anticommunist movement. He met secretly with Federal Bureau of Investigation agents to pass along the names of people in Hollywood he suspected of communist activities. He was not required to provide evidence to support his accusations. Reagan voiced his concerns about commu-

nism in Hollywood in testimony before the House Committee on Un-American Activities, the congressional committee established to investigate U.S. public officials and private citizens alleged to be communists. He also founded a group to verify that political candidates were suitably anticommunist.

Given his strong opposition to communism and taxation, Reagan's political views most closely matched those of the more conservative Republican Party. But despite his views, Reagan was a registered Democrat until 1962. As a young man, Reagan had been a strong supporter of President Franklin Roosevelt, and of

Ronald Reagan accused Soviet dictator Joseph Stalin of attempting to use Hollywood as a vehicle to spread communist ideas in America.

the giant government programs that helped end the Great Depression.

Reagan's movie career faded in the 1950s. After working briefly at a nightclub in Las Vegas, in 1954 he signed a contract with General Electric (GE) to introduce a weekly television show the company sponsored, and give speeches in its factories as part of a community relations campaign.

Reagan used these numerous speaking opportunities—he gave an estimated nine thousand speeches during his eight years with GE—as a forum to express his patriotic, anticommunist, and probusiness political views. Government, he claimed in his speeches, had become too big and bothersome and was infringing on the rights of individual Americans and corporations. These themes would continue

to dominate his speeches throughout his political career.

Though his association with the company ended in 1962, Reagan's highly visible role as a GE spokesman established him as a leading conservative voice. He gained further stature by giving more than two hundred speeches in support of Republican candidate Richard Nixon's unsuccessful bid for the presidency in 1960. Reagan's conservatism and national prominence made him a natural ally for 1964 presidential candidate and extreme conservative Barry Goldwater. In the last days of Goldwater's failed campaign, Reagan reached a national audience with a televised speech later entitled "A Time for Choosing."

Reagan's speech—a spirited defense of private property rights and the American

During the 1964 presidential campaign, Reagan (left) supported fellow conservative Barry Goldwater (right).

CAMPAIGNING FOR GOLDWATER

Reagan gained national recognition for his 1964 televised address on behalf of Presidential candidate Barry Goldwater. Early in the speech, reproduced in Speaking My Mind, *Reagan states his support for the war in Vietnam. He goes on to address some of his favorite themes: patriotism, personal freedom, and the need for a smaller government.*

"We are at war with the most dangerous enemy that has ever faced mankind in his long climb from the swamp to the stars, and it has been said that if we lose that war, and in so doing lose this way of freedom of ours, history will record with the greatest astonishment that those who had the most did the least to prevent its happening. Well, I think it's time we ask ourselves if we still know the freedoms that were intended for us by the founding fathers. . . .

You and I are told increasingly that we have to choose between a left or a right, but I would like to suggest that there is no such thing as a left or right. There is only up or down—up to man's age-old dream—the ultimate in individual freedom consistent with law and order—or down to the ant heap of totalitarianism. . . . [T]hose who would trade our freedom for security have embarked on this downward course. . . .

For three decades we have sought to solve the problems of unemployment through government planning, and the more the plans fail, the more the planners plan. . . . We have so many people who can't see a fat man standing beside a thin one without coming to the conclusion that the fat man got that way by taking advantage of the thin one! So they are going to solve all the problems of human misery through government and government planning. Well, now if government planning and welfare had the answer, and they've had almost thirty years of it, shouldn't we expect government to read the score to us once in a while? Shouldn't they be telling us about the decline each year in the number of people needing help? . . . the reduction in the need for public housing?

But the reverse is true. Each year the need grows greater, the program grows greater."

ideal of freedom, as well as an attack on high taxes and the failures of the national government—thrust him to the forefront of the Republican party and fired his own political aspirations. "You and I have a rendezvous with destiny," he told his audience. "We will preserve for our children this, the last best hope of man on earth, or we will sentence them to take the last step into a thousand years of darkness."[9]

At the urging of a handful of wealthy California conservatives, Reagan soon decided to test his political message in a run for public office. In January 1966 he announced his campaign for governor of California, and in November of that year he handily defeated his opponent, the Democratic candidate Edmund Brown. Reagan now had the opportunity to put his principles to the test as governor of a state that was suffering from tremendous economic problems.

In his two terms as governor, Reagan worked to build a solid record of political achievement. He and the state legislature increased funding for public schools, passed laws that were tough on crime, and enacted reforms in the welfare system that were widely seen as successful.

Reagan had less success in turning around the state's troubled economy. While he campaigned against higher taxes and bigger budgets, his fight against them once in office was unsuccessful. The state's annual budget more than doubled during his eight years as governor. To meet the state government's rising expenses, he ordered the largest tax increases in state history until that time.

While governor, Reagan kept a careful eye on national politics, awaiting his opportunity to seek higher office. His first run for president of the United States, in 1968, ended after he finished a distant third on the ballot at the Republican nominating convention. He made a more serious challenge for the nation's highest office in 1976. At the Republican convention, he lost to the incumbent president, Gerald Ford, by a narrow margin. As the 1980 elections approached, Reagan was almost seventy years of age. He was running out of time to win the nation's highest office.

REAGAN FOR PRESIDENT

From the start of his 1980 campaign, Reagan promised voters that he had a plan for solving America's problems. While he lacked his opponent President Carter's ability to master the details and subtleties of issues, he was a remarkably persuasive public speaker—a skill that earned him the nickname "the Great Communicator." He used straightforward language to describe the problems facing the country and to describe his solutions. "There are simple answers, but there are not always easy ones," he was fond of saying on the campaign trail.[10]

Many Americans responded well to Reagan's message, in part because the messenger believed it so firmly himself. His own journey from rags to riches was proof enough for him that America was the greatest country on earth. As he saw it, his role as president would be to share America's grand tradition of opportunity and freedom with the rest of the country. As he explained in his January 11, 1989 final address to the nation:

> I wasn't a great communicator, but I communicated great things, and they didn't spring full bloom from my brow, they came from the heart of a great nation—from our experience, our wisdom, and our belief in the

principles that have guided us for two centuries.[11]

Reagan's economic strategy was among the simple answers he presented to the American people. Reaganomics, as the plan came to be known, blamed overtaxation and the tremendous size and power of the federal government for the stagnant U.S. economy. His cure involved lower taxes and big cuts in federal programs, particularly in the social welfare programs that were intended to help poor Americans.

The basic principles of Reaganomics ran against the trends established by American presidents over the previous fifty years. Beginning in 1933 with Franklin Roosevelt's public works projects designed to pull the nation out of the Great Depression, government spending and programs had steadily increased. The growth intensified under Lyndon Johnson, who in the mid-1960s launched his "war on poverty" with massive public assistance programs including Medicare and Medicaid. Even conservative presidents such as Nixon and Eisenhower had spent huge amounts of federal funds on social programs. Reagan promised voters that he would reverse this trend.

Reagan also proposed large increases in military spending. A more powerful military, he maintained, was essential to prevent acts of aggression by the Soviet Union.

PREACHING PRIDE IN AMERICA

Reagan's economic plan met with a great deal of skepticism among both Democrats and Republicans. George Bush, his opponent for the Republican nomination, was one of many political opponents who doubted that a combination of lower taxes and increased defense spending was the solution to the nation's economic woes. Bush labeled Reagan's proposal "voodoo economics," implying that the plan was not based on sound economic principles.

But Reagan's attractiveness as a candidate had little to do with his ideas for solving specific economic problems; it had little to do with specific issues at all. Instead, Reagan's appeal to a renewed sense of patriotism proved to be far more persuasive to voters. After nearly two decades of economic and political misfortune, Americans wanted a president who promised to restore dignity and respect to the office and the nation. Reagan was well aware of the voting public's mood. As he later wrote in his 1990 autobiography:

During the summer and fall of 1980, there were many problems facing our nation: the tragic neglect of our military establishment, high unemployment and an ailing economy, the continuing expansion of Communism abroad, the taking of the hostages in Iran.

But to me none was more serious than the fact that America had lost faith in itself.

We were told there was a "malaise" in our nation and America was past its prime; we had to get used to less, and the American people were responsible for the problems we faced.

We were told we would have to lower our expectations; America would never

COURTING THE NEW RIGHT

The ultraconservative New Right movement was critical to Reagan's victory in the 1980 election. In the following conversations, excerpted from Deborah H. Strober and Gerald S. Strober's Reagan: The Man and His Presidency, *New Right leader Jerry Falwell discusses Reagan's close ties to the movement, as well as the strength of Falwell's group, the Moral Majority.*

"We were careful in those days to say we could not endorse or support a candidate under federal law, so we said, 'Just vote for the Reagan of your choice.' . . .

We planned a big meeting in Dallas in the summer of 1980. . . . Reagan came. We met with him ahead of time. I told him, 'We can't legally endorse you, but you can endorse us.' So that night, those were the words with which he started his speech. He said, 'I know that you can't legally endorse me, but I endorse you.' The place went wild. . . .

When we formed the Moral Majority, we had to break down the psychological barrier in the minds of most of the pastors that it is not wrong or unspiritual to be politically involved. We then had to register them to vote. We organized big campaigns and registered over eight million voters; we mobilized millions more who, although registered, were not voting. Eventually, in 1980, about 20 percent of the voters were Moral Majoritarians, and they voted for Reagan.

Eventually, about two hundred organizations were spun off the Moral Majority, including the Christian Coalition. We were there at the right time, at the right place. We had four tenets: pro-family, pro-life, pro-strong national defense, and pro-Israel. It didn't matter who you were, or where you went to church, or if you went to church or not. If you could say yes to the four tenets, you could be a part of it. There were millions out there who were ready for that."

again be as prosperous or have as bright a future as it once had.

Well, I disagreed with that.[12]

Reagan's response to the "malaise" was a campaign defined by its call for a return to traditional American values: patriotism, personal freedom and individualism, and strong family and moral values.

A campaign that focused on values and symbols instead of issues might have fallen flat in the hands of another candidate. But in Reagan, many Americans saw a patriot, a poised and confident leader, and an optimist who believed that America's best days were ahead. He became, according to journalist Elizabeth Drew, "a vessel into which a lot of people are pouring their ambitions . . . the telegenic, easy-going ex-actor in whom people are finding, or hoping to find, what they want."[13]

COURTING THE CONSERVATIVE VOTE

Reagan's 1980 campaign was perfectly timed to tap into a growing feeling of conservatism among the American people. National polls showed that many citizens agreed with his belief that the government had become too big to be effective. Resentment for the federal bureaucracy was building. And many Americans believed that the Soviet Union was now the dominant world military power.

No segment of the population reflected these sentiments better than what became known as the New Right. A powerful force on the American political landscape, the New Right was a coalition of people who held in common a concern about declining moral values at home and declining American prestige abroad. The coalition was born in the 1970s out of exasperation with the federal government, a reaction to liberal initiatives to gain legal protections for blacks, homosexuals, and women, and a stumbling economy.

The New Right's philosophy, and its pessimistic view of where the nation was headed, was clearly captured in the words of one of its leaders, James Robison of the James Robison Evangelistic Association in Texas:

> The divorce rate skyrockets, homes are crumbling, child abuse increases at a shocking rate, alcohol and drug abuse are rampant, the crime rate rises, and sexual immorality runs amok. America's star is sinking fast. If Christians don't begin immediately to assert their influence, it may be too late to save America from the destruction toward which it is plunging.[14]

The New Right's leadership sought to capitalize on the potential voting power of more than 40 million conservative, church-going, Christian Americans. The televangelist Jerry Falwell, a highly visible New Right leader, joined in the call for these voters to assert themselves as a political force:

> It is time that we come together, and rise up against the tide of permissiveness and moral decay that is crushing in on our nation from every side. . . . I am speaking about survival and calling upon those Americans who believe in decency and integrity to stand for what is good and what is right.[15]

The New Right echoed Reagan's call for increased pride in America, and a forceful anticommunist political stance. At the same time, the movement demanded a war on pornography and an amendment to the Constitution that would allow prayer in public schools. It was fiercely opposed to abortion, gay rights, feminism, and perceived threats to personal freedom such as gun control.

Reagan, seen here with Jerry Falwell (far left) and others, publicly announced his firm belief in God and prayer.

In Reagan, the movement had found a leader who would support its cause. As a young man in Illinois, Reagan was baptized into the local Christian church, where he taught Sunday school and led prayer sessions. He publicly stated that he prayed often throughout each day, as his mother had taught him. When he was elected governor of California he said that he wanted to guide the state according to Jesus' teachings, and twice asked the prominent religious leader Billy Graham to speak to the state legislature.

In the New Right, Reagan recognized a powerful new block of ultraconservative voters that could be reached through the televangelists' weekly broadcasts. In his speeches, he actively courted the New Right's votes, often highlighting his own belief in God and prayer. "If we have come to a time in the United States when the attempt to see traditional moral values reflected in public policy leaves one open to irresponsible charges," he told a New Right audience in Texas, "then the structure of our free society is under attack and the foundation of our freedom is threatened."[16]

THE REAGAN DEMOCRATS

The New Right's ability to get millions of dedicated conservatives to the polls was critical to Reagan's success in 1980. These votes alone would not have been enough to give him the election, however. To win the White House, Reagan had to attract other voters—including Democrats—who had more moderate political views.

Though Reagan's own political agenda was far from moderate, several factors helped him pull off this political balancing act. First, his Democratic opponent, the incumbent president Jimmy Carter, had become extremely unpopular. A 1980 poll showed that only one in five Americans

REAGAN'S INAUGURAL ADDRESS

In his 1981 inaugural address, reproduced in Speaking My Mind, *Reagan pledges to lead the country out of its economic troubles with a federal government that is smaller and more responsive to the needs of the people. He also states that America will not back down from the threat of communism.*

"These United States are confronted with an economic affliction of great proportions. We suffer from the longest and one of the worst sustained inflations in our national history. It distorts our economic decisions, penalizes thrift, and crushes the struggling young and the fixed-income elderly alike. It threatens to shatter the lives of millions of our people. . . . In this present crisis, government is not the solution to our problem; government is the problem. From time to time we've been tempted to believe that society has become too complex to be managed by self-rule, that government by an elite group is superior to government for, by, and of the people. Well, if no one among us is capable of governing himself, then who among us has the capacity to govern someone else? . . . Now, so there will be no misunderstanding, it's not my intention to do away with government. It is rather to make it work—work with us, not over us; to stand by our side, not ride on our back. Government can and must provide opportunity, not smother it; foster productivity, not stifle it. . . . As for the enemies of freedom, those who are potential adversaries, they will be reminded that peace is the highest aspiration of the American people. We will negotiate for it, sacrifice for it; we will not surrender for it, now or ever. Our forbearance should never be misunderstood. Our reluctance for conflict should not be misjudged as a failure of will. When action is needed to preserve our national security, we will act. We will maintain sufficient strength to prevail if need be, knowing that if we do so we have the best chance of never having to use that strength."

approved of the job Carter was doing as president. Many Americans were ready to vote for whoever was running against Carter, regardless of that candidate's political views.

At the same time, Reagan carefully tailored his public image. While his beliefs remained very conservative, he described them in terms that made them appear to be less so. He selected George Bush, a moderate Republican, as his vice-presidential running mate. Many of the people who voted for Reagan in 1980 were registered Democrats.

THE REAGAN REVOLUTION

Reagan easily defeated Jimmy Carter in the November 1980 elections, winning the electoral votes of forty-four states. Buoyed by his popularity, the Republicans gained twelve new seats to take majority control of the Senate and picked up thirty-three new seats in the House of Representatives. Leading liberal Democrats such as George McGovern of South Dakota and Warren Magnuson of Washington were swept out of office by the conservative tide.

The Republican victory was so convincing that some analysts called it the "Reagan Revolution." Reagan supporters celebrated in early 1981 and eagerly awaited the sweeping changes that the "revolution" would bring to America's economic and political landscape. After Reagan took the oath of office, he pledged that he would not disappoint his voters:

> Well, this administration's objective will be a healthy, vigorous, growing economy that provides equal opportunities for all Americans, with no barriers born of bigotry or discrimination. Putting America back to work means putting all Americans back to work. Ending inflation means freeing all Americans from the terror of runaway living costs. . . . With the idealism and fair play which are the core of our system and our strength, we can have a strong and prosperous America, at peace with itself and the world.[17]

Chapter

2 Reaganomics in Action

In November of 1980, shortly after he had won the presidential election, Ronald Reagan received a letter from former president Richard Nixon. Nixon first congratulated Reagan on his victory, and then offered advice:

> I am convinced that decisive action on the home front is by far the number one priority. Unless you are able to shape up our home base it will be almost impossible to conduct an effective foreign policy. Consequently, I would suggest that for at least six months you not travel abroad and that you focus all the attention of your appointees, the Congress and the people on your battle against inflation. . . . The time to take the heat for possibly unpopular budget cuts is in 1981, not 1982 or 1984.[18]

Reagan took Nixon's advice and made fixing the U.S. economy his top priority. In an address from the Oval Office a month after his inauguration, he warned that economic conditions were indeed dire. Inflation had risen to 13 percent in 1980 despite the government's best efforts to control it, and interest rates on borrowed money topped 20 percent in December of the same year. He asked Congress and the public to support his solution. "We must not be timid," he said. "We will restore the freedom of all men and women to excel and create. We will unleash the energy and genius of the American people, traits which have never failed us."[19]

Reagan announced his recovery plan on February 18 during a televised speech to a joint session of Congress. The plan had three essential parts, each firmly grounded in the principles of Reaganomics that he had advocated on the campaign trail. Taken together, Reagan predicted they would lower inflation and interest rates, and add 3 million new jobs.

First, Reagan proposed a drastic reduction in the tax rate. When individuals and corporations were taxed too much, Reagan believed, they were less likely to work hard or produce more. They were also less likely to save and invest, other key factors in a healthy economy. On the other hand, lower taxes would motivate people to work harder, because they would be allowed to keep a higher percentage of what they earned. Corporations would also have greater incentive to produce more and to create more jobs.

The second piece of Reagan's recovery plan was the removal of many federal restrictions on American corporations. Reagan argued that an overabundance of government rules and regulations were discouraging corporate growth. Freed from bureaucratic bonds, the president believed that the economy would return to health as businesses grew and employed more people.

Finally, Reagan called for dramatic cuts in the size of the federal government. Unnecessary federal employees and departments were wasting precious taxpayer dollars, he said. Wasteful social programs, especially those designed for the poor, would also have to be trimmed. Reagan believed that the benefits produced by a healthy economy, including more jobs

and higher wages, would flow down from the wealthiest to the poorest Americans—making welfare programs unnecessary except as a last resort. This idea caused critics to label his economic program "trickle-down" economics.

The essential ideas of Reaganomics were not new. Conservatives had long argued for smaller government programs and relaxed restrictions on corporations as a way of helping the economy. And in the 1970s, a young economist named Arthur Laffer theorized that cuts in the tax rate would actually lead to increased tax revenue, an idea that Reagan became quite attached to.

SLASHING TAXES

Soon after announcing his economic plan, Reagan introduced legislation in Congress asking that income taxes be slashed by 10 percent a year for three years, for a total cut of 30 percent. Congress eventually accepted a slightly modified proposal that cut taxes by 23 percent over three years.

The same bill also contained tax cuts for married couples and incentive programs to encourage saving and charitable contributions by individuals. The tax on unearned income—gains on investments in stocks, bonds, and real estate—was reduced, as was the bite that the government took out of inheritances.

Reagan argued that these tax cuts would ultimately help all Americans by reviving the economy. But in fact, the wealthiest segment of the population reaped most of the benefits of the tax re-

Reagan made the improvement of the United States' economy a large priority in his presidency.

THE DECISION TO SLASH TAXES

Donald Regan, who served as one of Reagan's chiefs of staff, explains in Deborah H. Strober and Gerald S. Strober's Reagan: The Man and His Presidency *why the president made cutting income taxes the top priority of his first term in office.*

"Reagan firmly believed that America needed a tax cut. He once told a story of how he first realized what taxes were doing to the American ethic. When he was in Hollywood, he would make about three or four hundred thousand dollars per picture. It took about three months to complete a picture. Reagan would work for three months, and loaf for three months, so he was making between six and seven hundred thousand dollars a year. Between Uncle Sam and the state of California, over 91 percent of that was taken by taxes. His question, asked rhetorically, was: 'Why should I have done a third picture, even if it was *Gone with the Wind?* What good would it have done me?'

So he loafed for a part of the year. And he said the same thing was happening throughout America. People would reach a certain peak, and then they weren't willing to do the extra effort that was needed to keep us a first-class nation.

He thought we should cut taxes; at that point we were in the 70 percent federal bracket. This was a priority of his; he got it passed in the first year. But I'm sorry to say that Bob Dole and others in Congress, under the lashing of the Democrats, kept whittling away at it as they saw the deficits increasing.

Rather than cut spending, they wanted to take back some of the tax cuts. Reagan was adamant on that; only as a very reluctant last resort, when he was convinced that Congress would go nowhere else, would he then agree to some tax increase in return for spending cuts."

duction. According to one study, the 31.7 percent of Americans making under $15,000 a year received just 8.5 percent of the tax cuts, while the 12.6 percent of people earning over $50,000 a year benefited from 35 percent of the cut.

Corporations also benefited tremendously from the new tax code. It was laden with special allowances and tax breaks for whole industries and corporations. After the plan was passed by Congress, the amount that corporations contributed via tax payments to the Federal government's coffers plummeted from 13 percent to 8 percent of the total.

SHRINKING GOVERNMENT

For Reaganomics to work, the loss of revenue caused by lower taxes had to be offset with cutbacks in federal spending. To accomplish this goal, the Reagan administration set out to eliminate the government programs and departments they believed were wasteful.

Nowhere did Reagan see more waste than in the social service programs designed to aid the poor. As he wrote in his diary, referring to former president Lyndon B. Johnson's establishment of social programs for the poor in the 1960s, "It was LBJ's war on poverty that led us to our present mess."[20]

The very idea behind these government programs ran contrary to Reagan's beliefs that, through hard work and perseverance, other Americans could make the same leap out of poverty that he had made as a young man in Illinois.

Government aid such as welfare, Aid for Families with Dependent Children, Medicaid, food stamps, and other programs, he reasoned, had a numbing effect. By giving the needy handouts without asking them to do anything in return, the government robbed them of incentives to change their condition. Martin Anderson, Reagan's first domestic policy advisor, described those requiring government aid: "Free from basic wants, but heavily dependent on the State, with little hope of breaking free, they are a new caste, the 'Dependent Americans.'"[21]

Reagan was adamant that government programs should be the safety net reserved for those who were not healthy enough to work, while those who were able to work were weaned off. He tried to break the cycle of dependence by making it more difficult for the poor to obtain government aid.

The administration put a cap on the total amount of benefits someone could receive, and as part of an $18 billion budget cut for Medicaid, government health coverage for low-income people. The cuts made it more difficult for the poor to retain hospital and health coverage. The food stamp program and Aid for Families with Dependent Children, designed to help low-income families, also suffered significant budget cuts. At the same time, Reagan shortened the period of eligibility for unemployment insurance, and supported a workfare program that would require the able-bodied poor to work in some capacity in return for their government checks.

Reagan's proposed cuts came under immediate attack from his political opponents. Speaker of the House Tip O'Neill, a Democrat, was astounded that the president wanted to trim programs for the needy while giving tax breaks to the wealthy. "The President might be a real tightwad when it comes to programs that help working families," said O'Neill, "but when it comes to giving tax breaks to the wealthy of this country, the president has a heart of gold."[22]

Reagan even attracted criticism from his own party. Marc Marks, a Republican con-

Speaker of the House Tip O'Neill was amazed that the president wanted to eliminate programs for the needy while giving tax breaks to the rich.

gressman from Pennsylvania, blasted the Reagan administration for being blind to:

> the wretchedness and to the suffering they are inflicting . . . on the sick, the poor, the handicapped, the blue collar, the white collar workers, the small business person, the black community, the community of minorities generally, women of all economic and social backgrounds, men and women who desperately need job training, families that deserve and desire the right to send their children to college or graduate school—in fact, anyone and everyone, other than those who have been fortunate enough to insulate themselves in a corporate suit of armor.[23]

But Reagan did not believe that he was cutting poor people off from programs they depended on. Instead, he believed he was setting them free from programs that were keeping them in poverty. He made this clear in a July 1981 speech to the National Association for the Advancement of Colored People.

> Many in Washington over the years have been more dedicated to making needy people government-dependent, rather than independent. They've created a new kind of bondage. Just as the Emancipation Proclamation freed black people 118 years ago, today we need to declare an economic emancipation.[24]

Overall, Reagan asked Congress for cuts of $40 billion in the 1982 budget, many of these coming from social welfare programs. He also recommended that the amount of budget cuts grow to $100 billion in 1986. After fierce debate, Congress gave him almost everything he requested.

DEREGULATION

As Reagan's first year in office progressed, his efforts to curb the size and influence of the federal government gained momentum. He announced a plan to eliminate three hundred thousand federal jobs, and proposed that the states assume many of the responsibilities formerly shouldered by the federal government, including the food stamp and welfare programs.

Reagan also pursued his goal of a smaller, simpler government through deregulation, the removal of regulations on

BUILDING AMERICA'S MILITARY MIGHT

In his autobiography, Reagan explains why he wanted to increase military spending even while trying to cut government spending in other areas.

"I sent to Congress a bill calling for an across-the-board thirty-percent tax cut over three years. Meanwhile, we launched a program under Vice President Bush to reduce unnecessary government regulation of the economy. After the broadcast, Tip O'Neill and other tax-and-spenders in Congress let out a howl and I knew we were in for a battle. A few days later, we unveiled a plan to cut billions of federal expenditures by eliminating needless boards, agencies, and programs—a start at reducing the $80 billion budget deficit the federal government faced that year—and the Democrats let out another howl and proposed drastic cuts in defense spending. Well, I was determined to *increase* military spending to reverse the effects of years of neglect of our armed services.

Pentagon leaders told me appalling stories of how the Soviets were gaining on us militarily, both in nuclear and conventional forces; they were spending fifty percent more each year on weapons than we were; meanwhile, in our armed forces, the paychecks were so small that some married enlisted men and women were eligible for welfare benefits; many military personnel were so ashamed of being in the service that as soon as they left their posts, they put on civilian clothes.

I told the Joint Chiefs of Staff that I wanted to do whatever it took to make our men and women proud to wear their uniforms again . . . I wanted a balanced budget. But I also wanted peace through strength."

industry to encourage economic growth. The effects of deregulation were felt in almost every government department.

The Labor Department trimmed down by firing employees and shrinking its job training program. The Department of Energy and Nuclear Regulatory Commission relaxed their oversight of nuclear power plants. At the same time, the National Highway Traffic Safety Administration announced a plan to delay or eliminate thirty-four car safety regulations, including those that would require air bags, lower emissions, and better fuel economy. In every case, the elimination of standards was meant to make it easier and less expensive for private industry to function.

At other agencies, the cutbacks were even more severe. Environmental Protection Agency head Anne Gorsuch Burford reduced her own budget and staff, and eased federal air and water pollution standards. The situation was similar in the Department of the Interior, the agency with primary responsibility for managing the nation's natural resources. Secretary of the Interior James Watt let it be known early in his tenure that his department would allow corporations to "drill more, mine more, cut more timber" on federal lands, and opened up protected areas to coal mining, logging, recreation, and offshore oil drilling.[25]

WAITING FOR IMPROVEMENTS

The American people had been more than willing to place the blame for their economic troubles at the federal government's feet, and they responded well to Reagan's promise of reform. One poll taken soon after the plan was announced found that two-thirds of Americans approved of Reagan's recommended economic cure.

But in spite of Reagan's sweeping reforms, the economy got worse before it got better. In 1982, the deepest recession since World War II befell the United States. Eleven million people found themselves out of work—almost one in ten

Americans—and 4.6 million Americans applied for unemployment benefits, the highest number since the program started in 1935.

As the recession worsened, the poverty rate climbed to its highest level in twenty years. One in five blacks was unemployed, and 2.5 million Americans were homeless. The social programs that Reagan detested were needed more than ever before.

The recession *did* have the positive effect of slowing the rate of inflation. But interest rates, another key indicator of economic health, remained over 16 percent. Most disturbingly, economists projected a $500 billion deficit over the next

Thousands of homeless Americans crowd onto the grounds of the capitol to receive a traditional Thanksgiving meal. The poverty rate climbed during Reagan's term.

three years. The balanced budget and robust economy that Reagan predicted in his 1981 State of the Union address seemed far off indeed.

In an article published in *The Atlantic Monthly* in December 1981, Reagan's own budget director, David Stockman, admitted that he knew before the Reagan plan was even sent to Congress for approval that it would not work. Lower taxes just did not add up to greater revenue for the government, he said, before making his own prediction of record-setting deficits in the years to come.

Many critics agreed with Stockman's opinion that the numbers did not add up. First, the cuts Reagan proposed in nondefense spending were offset by the massive increase in military spending that he requested and that Congress approved. Out of a total 1982 budget of $757 billion, for example, $221 billion was earmarked for defense spending.

Reagan's failure to make major changes to the enormously expensive Social Security program was the second factor in his inability to balance the budget. The program, which was established in 1935 to provide income to retired people, consumed nearly half of the federal budget. Yet even with this massive infusion of cash from the government, enormous shortfalls were projected early in the next century. Although Reagan was well aware of the problems that Social Security faced, trimming the program was politically dangerous. Elderly Americans did not want to lose the benefits, and they made sure that their Congressional representatives were well aware of their con-

cerns. As a result, the changes that Reagan finally made in 1983 were far less than were needed.

Just as Stockman and other experts predicted, the combination of tax cuts, defense spending, and a draining Social Security program led to staggering federal deficits. The government spent $111 billion more than it made in 1982. By 1985, the budget deficit would swell to $245 billion.

PREACHING PATIENCE

Even as the public grumbled under the weight of the recession, and Democrats harped on the ineffectiveness of Reaganomics, Reagan asked for patience. "We have made a new beginning, but we have only begun," he said in January of 1982. His 1983 budget held more of the same strong medicine, including additional cuts of $26 billion in social programs. He promised that his program would "put us on the road to prosperity and stable growth by the latter half of this year."[26] Reagan also asked the public to show faith in his programs, and blamed liberal skeptics and the media for standing in the way of a recovery.

In a time of recession like this, there's a great element of psychology in economics. And you can't turn on the evening news without seeing that they're going to interview someone else who has just lost his job or they're outside the factory gate that has laid off workers—the constant down-beat that can contribute psychologically to slowing down a new

HANDS-ON LEADERSHIP?

"Again, contrary to the usual image, the personal leadership of the President was indispensable to the program's success. When the effort was launched, worries about lost revenue dominated Hill discussions—particularly from Dole and Domenici on the Republican side, but also, of course, from the Democratic leadership in the House. In the spring and early summer of 1981, doubts were rampant as to whether the program could be adopted at all.

But when Democratic prophecies of defeat were brought to the White House by the leadership team, or by Howard Baker, the President always gave the same answer: "Do what is necessary to get the program adopted. Don't back off. Find out what needs doing and do it. Period." In White House meetings day after day, that message came through loud and clear. The President had supplied the conceptual basis of the program, and now he was throwing into the battle his communication skills to explain it to the public and the political will to stay the course until the plan was adopted.

Given his courage and steadfastness, which I have witnessed in many similar circumstances, I am certain the tax reduction program would not have been adopted under any other President in recent memory. Ronald Reagan, working through his aides and directly with Congress, showed again that behind that pleasant demeanor there was a tough and determined man."

recovery that is in the offing. Is it news that some fellow out in South Succotash someplace has just been laid off . . . or someone's complaint that budget cuts are going to hurt their present program?[27]

Despite his optimistic public statements, Reagan was concerned about the persistently poor economic conditions. While he on one hand promised that he would never "balance the budget on the backs of the American taxpayers," he

THE ASSASSINATION ATTEMPT

In March of 1981, John Hinckley Jr. attempted to assassinate President Reagan outside of a Washington hotel. Reagan describes the attack in his 1990 autobiography.

"After the speech, I left the hotel through a side entrance and passed a line of press photographers and TV cameras. I was almost to the car when I heard what sounded like two or three firecrackers over to my left—just a small fluttering sound, *pop, pop, pop.*

I turned and said, "What the hell's that?"

Just then, Jerry Parr, the head of our Secret Service unit, grabbed me by the waist and literally hurled me into the back of the limousine. I landed on my face atop the arm rest across the backseat and Jerry jumped on top of me. When he landed, I felt a pain in my upper back that was unbelievable. It was the most excruciating pain I had ever felt.

'Jerry,' I said, 'get off, I think you've broken one of my ribs.'

John Hinckley, Jr.'s bullet probably caught me in midair at the same moment I was being thrown into the back of the car by Jerry Parr. After they took it out of me, I saw the bullet. It looked like a nickel that was black on one side; it had been flattened into a small disc and darkened by the paint of the limousine. First the bullet had struck the limousine, then it had ricocheted through the small gap between the body of the car and the door hinges. It hit me under my left arm, where it made a small slit like a knife wound.

I'd always been told that no pain is as excruciating as a broken bone; that's why I thought Jerry had broken my rib when he landed so hard on me. But it wasn't Jerry's weight I felt; according to the doctors, the flattened bullet had hit my rib edgewise, then turned over like a coin, tumbling down through my lung and stopping less than an inch from my heart."

asked Congress in 1982 to approve a tax increase of $100 billion over three years.[28] It was the largest tax hike in American history.

A slim victory by the Democrats in the 1982 congressional elections indicated that people were not heeding the president's pleas for patience. Reagan, however, remained upbeat. "We still have a long way to go," he announced in September of that year, even as the economy continued to slumber, "but together we have pulled America back from the brink of disaster."[29]

DECISIVE LEADERSHIP

Regardless of how well his policies were actually working, Reagan always appeared to be optimistic and firmly in command. From the very beginning of his presidency, he was the confident, decisive leader that his predecessor Carter was not, and many Americans loved him for that alone.

In August 1981, when thirteen thousand air traffic controllers went on strike, Reagan ordered them, as government employees, back to work. When they refused to report for work, he fired them all—although it would prove enormously expensive and difficult to hire and train replacements, and the loss of such an experienced crew of workers posed a real threat to airline safety. But the message to the American people was clear: Reagan was in command, and he would move quickly and decisively on matters of national and international importance.

THE ASSASSINATION ATTEMPT

On March 30, 1981, a mentally disturbed young drifter named John Hinckley almost put an end to Reagan's presidency.

In early 1981 Reagan was shot during an assassination attempt. His positive outlook on the situation led to his quick recovery and the public's respect and admiration.

Outside of a hotel in Washington, D.C., Hinckley fired six bullets at the president. One round ricocheted off a car, entered Reagan's chest, and lodged within an inch of his heart. Three other members of his staff were wounded, including his press secretary, James Brady.

A Secret Service agent threw himself over the president as soon as the shots were fired and shoved him into a waiting limousine. Reagan did not realize he had been shot at first and walked into the hospital under his own power. Doctors later said that if he had had to wait five minutes for treatment he would have died.

Reagan remained upbeat and good-humored in the hospital despite the severity of his wound. In the emergency room, he borrowed a phrase from the legendary boxer Jack Dempsey, saying to his wife, "Honey, I forgot to duck."[30] Before he underwent surgery, he jokingly asked the surgeons if they were all Republicans.

His humor and courage throughout the ordeal endeared him to many Americans. In public opinion polls, his approval rating soared higher than any president in history. Buoyed by the public support, he was back on Capitol Hill just one month later, successfully lobbying Congress to implement his economic reforms.

By the end of 1982, Reagan and a cooperative Congress had put in place the legislative and political pieces that he believed would lead to an economic recovery. The president then turned his attention to the most critical issue of foreign policy that he would face—dealing with the Soviet Union.

Chapter

3 The Cold Warrior

From the end of World War II to the Reagan presidency, the relationship between the United States and the Soviet Union had been deeply troubled. The roots of the split lay in differing political beliefs and economic systems. As Communists, the Soviets believed in government ownership of factories, machines, banks, and land. The needs of the society were seen as more important than those of individuals, and political freedom was restricted. On the other hand, the U.S. economy is based on capitalism, in which industries and land are usually privately owned. America's democratic system of government allows individuals to disagree with the government and express their political views.

While the Soviet Union and the United States joined forces to defeat Germany in World War II, tension and distrust grew quickly in the late 1940s. The first major disagreement between the capitalist, democratic western nations led by the United States and the Communist nations led by the Soviet Union was over the control of a defeated Germany following the war. Unable to agree on a plan for a unified Germany, the occupying powers split the country into two pieces; one controlled by the Soviets and the other by the United States and its allies.

The 1950s and 1960s were marked by intense economic competition, strained diplomatic relations, and massive military buildups on both sides—a state of affairs that was known as the Cold War. Communications between the two sides dropped to a minimum, and each side greeted the other's actions with suspicion and fear. The United States built anticommunist alliances with other nations around the world and focused its foreign policy on stopping the spread of communism. Meanwhile, the Soviet Union kept a tight political and economic grip on its allies. The Soviets also attempted to spread communism around the world, supporting communist takeovers of China, North Vietnam, and Cuba.

MUTUAL ASSURED DESTRUCTION

The greatest danger stemming from poor Soviet-U.S. relations was the threat of nuclear war. For a brief period in the late 1940s the United States and its allies had a monopoly on nuclear weapons. They used this advantage to counter the threat of a

Soviet invasion of Europe. But the Soviets quickly built their own deadly arsenal, and by the mid-1950s, the chance of global nuclear war had become a deadly concern. The risky political strategy that kept the United States and the Soviet Union from using their nuclear weapons was called mutual assured destruction, or MAD.

MAD was based on the belief that neither side would ever start a nuclear war if they knew that the other side had enough fire power to wipe them out as well. For MAD to work, both nations had to have the ability to obliterate each other regardless of who fired first. If one side was seen as gaining a distinct military advantage, the balance of peace was threatened.

As a result, the United States and the Soviet Union spent billions of dollars matching each other missile for missile. Each side had enough weapons to destroy the opposition hundreds of times over.

REAGAN'S ANTI-SOVIET RHETORIC

Reagan's 1982 speech before the British Parliament was a perfect example of the hard line he took toward the Soviet Union early in his presidency. In this passage from Speaking My Mind, *he accuses the Communist nation of pushing the world toward a nuclear war.*

"Historians looking back at our time will note the consistent restraint and peaceful intentions of the West. They will note that it was the democracies who refused to use the threat of their nuclear monopoly in the forties and early fifties for territorial or imperial gain. Had the nuclear monopoly been in the hands of the Communist world, the map of Europe—indeed, the world—would look very different today. And certainly they will note it was not the democracies that invaded Afghanistan or suppressed Polish Solidarity or used chemical and toxic warfare in Afghanistan and Southeast Asia.

If history teaches anything, it teaches self-delusion in the face of unpleasant facts is folly. We see around us today the marks of our terrible dilemma—predictions of doomsday, antinuclear demonstrations, an arms race in which the West must, for its own protection, be an unwilling participant. At the same time we see totalitarian forces in the world who seek subversion and conflict around the globe to further their barbarous assault on the human spirit. What, then, is our course? Must civilization perish in a hail of fiery atoms? Must freedom wither in a quiet, deadening accommodation with totalitarian evil?"

Even if superior Soviet weapons were able to wipe out America's land-based missiles, for example, the United States could respond using the three thousand nuclear warheads it had hidden on submarines at sea.

CUBAN MISSILE CRISIS

The two nations reached the very brink of nuclear war during the Cuban Missile Crisis of October 1962. The crisis erupted after the Soviet Union deployed nuclear missiles in the communist nation of Cuba, just ninety miles from Florida. President Kennedy viewed the installation of the missiles as a deliberately provocative act by the Soviets and threatened to respond with military intervention. The Soviets, confronted by overwhelming military force, finally agreed to withdraw their missiles from Cuba.

Moments of high tension were followed by periods of détente, a term used to describe the relaxation of tensions during which the two nations and their allies managed to peacefully coexist through a series of trade and arms control agreements. Presidents Nixon, Ford, and Carter practiced the policy of détente with varying degrees of success. In 1972, Nixon and Soviet leader Leonid Brezhnev signed the Strategic Arms Limitation Treaty (SALT) that froze the number of ballistic missiles the two countries held. President Carter and Brezhnev signed a second arms control agreement, SALT II, in 1979. The United States also began to export grain and other goods to aid the troubled Soviet economy.

Although past presidents had achieved some success in dealing with Soviet leader Leonid Brezhnev, when Reagan entered office the two nations were at a diplomatic low point.

For most of the 1970s, a measure of civility was maintained between the two nations, while presidents Nixon, Ford, and Carter attempted to move arms reduction negotiations forward. But in 1979, the Soviet army entered Afghanistan to wipe out rebels that threatened the Soviet-backed government. Furious at the invasion, President Carter ended grain shipment to the Soviets, and killed any chance that the SALT II treaty had of being approved by Congress. By the time Reagan entered office, political relations between the United States and the Soviet Union were as cold as they had ever been.

Tough Talk and Increasing Tension

A key event early in Reagan's first term drove the United States and the Soviets even further apart. In 1981, a powerful Polish independence movement led by a trade union called Solidarity was chipping away at the thirty-five-year-old Soviet-backed Communist government, and the Russians asked the Polish army to crack down on the revolutionaries. This move prompted harsh words from Reagan:

> I want to emphatically state tonight that if the outrages in Poland do not cease, we cannot and will not conduct business as usual with the perpetrators and those who aid and abet them. Make no mistake, their crime will cost them dearly in their future dealings with America and free peoples everywhere. I do not make this statement lightly or without serious reflection.[31]

Privately, he told Brezhnev that if Moscow continued to pressure the Polish army to react forcefully to the Solidarity movement, it would threaten relations between the two superpowers. Brezhnev ignored Reagan's objections and told the president that the matter was not the United States' concern.

As Soviet-U.S. relations took a turn for the worse, public protests against nuclear weapons were growing in size and strength. A Nuclear Freeze Movement demonstration drew five hundred thousand people to New York's Central Park in the summer of 1982. In Europe, antinuclear activists protested against the decision to place more American missiles on their continent.

A poll taken in 1982 found that 57 percent of Americans wanted an immediate nuclear weapons freeze by the United States and the Soviet Union. In 1982, the House of Representatives introduced a resolution in favor of a nuclear weapons

Demonstrators march to Central Park in New York in the summer of 1982 to support nuclear disarmament.

freeze. That fall, as testimony to the growing anxiety worldwide, more than 100 million people tuned in to *The Day After*, a television movie depicting the horrific destruction of a nuclear war.

PEACE THROUGH STRENGTH

The roots of Reagan's personal animosity toward the Soviet Union were as old as the Cold War itself. But the president's hatred for the Soviets and communism did not blind him to the dangers of nuclear war. He clearly understood the frightening absurdity of mutual assured destruction, and described it to a reporter in a 1989 interview:

> It's like you and me sitting here in a discussion where we were each pointing a loaded gun at each other and if you say anything wrong or I say anything wrong, we're going to pull the trigger. And I just thought this was ridiculous—mutual assured destruction. It really was a mad policy.[32]

He also believed the biblical prophecy of Armageddon, or the end of the world, to be literally true, and feared that nuclear war was the catastrophe that would cause it. These factors made him keenly interested in negotiating arms control agreements with the Soviets. But he wanted the agreements to come on his own terms.

Reagan believed that détente, as practiced in the 1970s, had been a failure. A decade of negotiations had produced few results, he argued, and treaties like SALT II had actually allowed the Soviets to pull ahead in the arms race. As president, he decided to pursue a strategy that involved less talk and more weapons—"peace through strength," he called it.

> We cannot negotiate arms control agreements that will slow down the Soviet military buildup as we let the Soviets move ahead of us in every category of armaments. . . . Once we clearly demonstrate to the Soviet leadership that we are determined to compete, arms control negotiations will again have a chance.[33]

Reagan's strategy to bring the Soviets to the bargaining table was to build weapons as quickly as he could. He embarked on the largest peacetime military buildup in history—and killed any chance he had at balancing the federal budget in the process.

The list of weapons funded by the Reagan administration is lengthy: the neutron bomb, nuclear artillery shells, Trident submarines, MX and Pershing II missiles, B-1 bombers, and B-2 stealth bombers, to name a few. Each one of these items came with an enormous price tag, and from 1981 to 1985 the defense budget soared from $171 billion to over $360 billion.

As Reagan shifted the arms race into high gear, the Soviets did their best to match the U.S. pace, warhead for warhead. The Soviets were forced to divert billions of dollars into their weapons program, putting pressure on the already shaky Soviet economy. Reagan hoped that the weight of more military spending on the Soviets would drive them to seek negotiations.

The Burden of the Presidency

As president, Reagan was responsible for deciding whether to launch America's missiles in the event of a nuclear war. In his autobiography, he discusses the tremendous weight of that responsibility.

"On inauguration day, after being briefed a few days earlier on what I was to do if it ever became necessary to unleash American nuclear weapons, I'd taken over the greatest responsibility of my life—of any human being's life. From then on, wherever I went, I carried a small plastic-covered card with me, and a military aide with a very specialized job was always close by. He or she carried . . . a small bag everyone referred to as 'the football.' It contained the directives for launching our nuclear weapons in retaliation for a nuclear attack on our country. The plastic-coated card, which I carried in a small pocket in my coat, listed the codes I would issue to the Pentagon confirming that it was actually the president of the United States who was ordering the unleashing of our nuclear weapons.

The decision to launch the weapons was mine alone to make.

We had many contingency plans for responding to a nuclear attack. But everything would happen so fast that I wondered how much planning or reason could be applied in such a crisis. The Russians sometimes kept submarines off our East Coast with nuclear missiles that could turn the White House into a pile of radioactive rubble within six or eight minutes.

Six minutes to decide how to respond to a blip on a radar scope and decide whether to unleash Armageddon! How could anyone apply reason at a time like that?"

Slow Steps Toward the Bargaining Table

As public and political pressure to end the arms race mounted, Reagan began to show more interest in negotiations with the Soviets. In a televised press conference in the spring of 1982, Reagan stated emphatically that he was committed to peace with the Soviets: "a nuclear war cannot be won and must never be fought. So, to those who protest against nuclear war, I can only say, I'm with you."[34]

In May, during a speech at his alma mater, Eureka College in Illinois, Reagan said that he was ready to have a personal meeting with Soviet leader Leonid Brezhnev to discuss "dismantling the nuclear menace":

> I hope we could arrange a future meeting where positive results can be anticipated. And when we sit down, I will tell President Brezhnev that the United States is ready to build a new understanding. . . . I will tell him that his government and his people have nothing to fear from the United States.[35]

He went on to propose arms reduction talks aimed at reducing both sides' land-based ballistic missiles by one-third.

The speech represented a dramatic change in tone from Reagan's usual expressions of distrust and distaste for the Soviets. On a trip to Europe in June, he described nuclear weapons as a threat to mankind and repeated his call for arms control talks. The Soviets responded to Reagan's peace overtures. In June of 1982, the first talks aimed at limiting nuclear arms in over three years got underway in Geneva, Switzerland.

The first issue under discussion in Geneva was the fate of intermediate-range nuclear weapons in Europe. Since the late 1970s, the presence of Soviet medium-range missiles aimed at Europe had been one of the United States' biggest concerns. Fearful of a nuclear attack that would take just minutes to reach European targets, the United States had responded by placing its own missiles there.

Reagan's proposal at Geneva was called the "zero option" and required that all intermediate-range Soviet weapons in Europe be removed; in return, the U.S.

would not deploy any more Pershing or cruise missiles on the continent.

The proposal amounted to a weapons-building freeze by the United States in return for a reduction in the Soviet arsenal. It required the Soviets to remove weapons already in place, while the United States had only to refrain from deploying new missiles. Reagan's own secretary of state, Alexander Haig, privately protested that the proposal did not give the Soviets enough negotiating room.

The second issue on the table was the plan, previously announced by Reagan in

In his Eureka College address, Reagan proposed a one-third reduction of land-based missiles in the Soviet Union and the United States. The public criticized this plan.

his Eureka College address, to limit long-range ballistic missiles. Because the Soviets had more land-based missiles than the United States, Reagan's proposed one-third reduction would have resulted in a larger bite out of the Soviet nuclear arsenal, and Brezhnev immediately rejected the proposal as another attempt by the United States to gain a military advantage.

Critics at home accused Reagan of introducing arms control proposals that he knew the Soviet Union would not agree to in order to cultivate his image as a leader who was truly interested in peace. According to one detractor, Senator Alan Cranston, the president's arms control effort was nothing more than "a public-relations campaign designed to persuade skeptics at home and abroad that he is committed to achieving equitable nuclear-arms reductions with the Soviet Union."[36]

STAR WARS

While arms negotiations inched forward, Reagan redoubled his commitment to building up the American military, asking

---

LAUNCHING THE STAR WARS PROGRAM

In a televised speech on March 23, 1983, Reagan announced his intention to build the Strategic Defense Initiative, an anti-missile shield that he hoped would protect the U.S. and alter the balance of power in the Cold War. As reprinted in his autobiography,

"Wouldn't it be better to save lives than to avenge them? . . . After careful consultation with my advisors, including the Joint Chiefs of Staff, I believe there is a way. Let me share with you a vision of the future which offers hope. It is that we embark on a program to counter the awesome Soviet missile threat with measures that are defensive. . . . What if free people could live secure in the knowledge that their security did not rest upon the threat of instant U.S. retaliation to deter a Soviet attack, that we could intercept and destroy strategic ballistic missiles before they reached our own soil or that of our allies? . . . I am directing a comprehensive and intensive effort to define a long-term research and development program to begin to achieve our ultimate goal of eliminating the threat posed by strategic nuclear missiles. This could pave the way for arms control measures to eliminate the weapons themselves. We seek neither military superiority nor political advantage. Our only purpose—one all people share—is to search for ways to reduce the danger of nuclear war."

Congress to spend $5.8 billion on nuclear weapons in 1983, a 40 percent increase over his 1981 request. At the same time, the president was looking in an entirely different direction for an edge against the Soviets.

In March 1983, he announced his intention to spend billions of dollars on the Strategic Defense Initiative (SDI), an antimissile shield that he hoped would render Soviet nuclear weapons useless. For Reagan, the SDI program, or Star Wars as it was soon nicknamed, represented a possible end to the menace of mutual assured destruction:

> Wouldn't it be better to save lives than to avenge them? . . . Let me share with you a vision of the future which offers hope. It is that we embark on a program to counter the awesome Soviet missile threat with measures that are defensive. . . . What if free people could live secure in the knowledge that their security did not rest upon the threat of instant U.S. retaliation to deter a Soviet attack, that we could intercept and destroy strategic ballistic missiles before they reached our own soil or that of our allies? . . . I call upon the scientific community, those who gave us nuclear weapons, to turn their great talents now to the cause of mankind and world peace, to give us the means of rendering these nuclear weapons impotent and obsolete.[37]

From the beginning, the Star Wars program was plagued by controversy and development problems. Critics argued that it was a violation of the 1972 Anti-Ballistic Missile Treaty signed by Nixon and Brezhnev. At the same time many people, including Reagan's senior military advisors, doubted that such a system could work. The system depended on unproven technology and, given the destructive power of a single nuclear warhead, it had to be perfect. Stopping nine out of ten missiles would not be good enough.

Many experts believed that the Star Wars program was another strategy to get the Soviets to the negotiating table. They believed that the Soviet Union, in an attempt to develop its own version of the expensive program, would cripple its own economy and be forced to bargain with the United States. Still others feared that an effective antimissile system would make the United States more likely to start a war, by improving the chances of an American "victory." To these critics, the launch of the Star Wars program was an aggressive act that the Soviets might respond to by building enough missiles to overcome any defense system.

THINGS FALL APART

As the negotiations in Geneva wore on without success, the level of distrust between the United States and the Soviet Union began to rise. Just a few weeks before Brezhnev died in November 1982, he accused Reagan of "threatening to push the world into the flames of nuclear war," and then promised that the Soviet Union would build up its military "with due account of the latest achievements of science and art of war."[38]

Doubts About Star Wars

William J. Crowe, chairman of the Joint Chiefs of Staff under Reagan, expresses in Deborah H. Strober and Gerald S. Strober's Reagan: The Man and His Presidency *the doubt that he and other military leaders shared about the potential of the SDI, or Star Wars, to defend the United States from a nuclear missile attack.*

"The reason the president was so adamant on SDI was that [Secretary of Defense Caspar] Weinberger had told him all that stuff; Weinberger was a fanatic on SDI.

The Chiefs had a little bit different view on the matter. It's not that we were against SDI, but we thought, one, that it was a very, very challenging technical problem, and that we were a long way from solving any of that stuff; we were really in an experimental mode. But in order to satisfy Weinberger and the president, [chief of the SDI program James] Abrahamson spent a lot of time talking as if the damn thing was in the parking lot. But it wasn't in the parking lot at all.

The Chiefs were suspicious of anything with so many uncertainties, with so many problems in developing. They spent an incredible amount of money on this. The Chiefs felt that we ought to go slow and see if the technical problems were amenable to a solution.

Before I left, it was obvious we could shoot down a missile, barring other complications. Whether we could weaponize the SDI, and whether we could afford the SDI, was never obvious while I was chairman. And we thought both of those questions should be explored in great depth before we went too damn far.

But there were a lot of people pushing hard for SDI— just push, push, push, spend, spend, spend, let's get it! They really thought we would really have a defense that would stop a missile. It was never clear to the Chiefs that we could build the kind of defense they were talking about."

Reagan's own words and actions were aggressive. In a March 1983 speech to the National Association of Evangelicals, he described the Soviet Union as "an evil empire" and "the focus of evil in the modern world."[39] Kenneth Adelman, the newly appointed head of the American arms negotiation team, shared his view. According to one White House staff member, Adelman viewed "the Russians as the very personification of evil itself, and it's very hard, if you have that view, to negotiate with them."[40]

The United States went ahead with the deployment of its new Pershing II intermediate-range missiles in Europe, and then a tragedy occurred that drove tensions even higher. In September 1983, a Korean Air Lines passenger flight mistakenly veered into Soviet airspace. The Soviets reacted by shooting it down without warning, killing the 269 civilians aboard. Again, Reagan responded with harsh words, accusing the Soviets of a deliberate "act of barbarism."[41]

In the wake of these events, arms control negotiations finally broke off in 1983. It would be two tension-filled years before the Soviet Union and the United States returned to the bargaining table.

4 Trouble Abroad

Reagan's first term in office had begun with a dramatic foreign policy success. On the day he was sworn in, Iran agreed to release the fifty-two American hostages it held in return for a U.S. pledge to release Iranian assets held in Western banks. It was a welcome end to a crisis that had held the nation's attention for 444 days, despite President Carter's attempts at economic, diplomatic, and even military intervention.

Unfortunately, the threat of terrorism to Americans abroad would rise throughout the 1980s. Terrorism had first entered the international spotlight at the 1972 Olympics in West Germany, when Palestinian radicals held eleven Israeli athletes hostage. All of the hostages and terrorists were killed in a shootout with West German police. As the 1970s continued, bombings, hijackings, and hostage-taking became more common, and Americans abroad were increasingly targeted because they were the most vulnerable representatives of a nation whose foreign policies were often unpopular.

Another troubling development was the growth of state-sponsored terrorism—terrorism that was supported or carried out by a hostile foreign government rather than by an isolated group of radicals or revolutionaries. Libya, Iran, Syria, and other nations supplied anti-American terrorists with money, weapons, training, protection, and passports. The primary goal of the terrorists and their supporters was to force the United States to alter its policies in the Middle East.

Reagan believed that the Soviet Union, as part of its effort to spread communism, was ultimately behind almost every terrorist group around the world. "Let us not delude ourselves," he said during his 1980 campaign. "The Soviet Union underlies all the unrest that is going on. If they weren't engaged in this game of dominoes, there wouldn't be any hot spots in the world."[42] Firm in this conviction, Reagan's attempts to combat global terrorism fit neatly into his overriding foreign policy concern—stamping out Soviet influence around the world.

LIBYA

One of the leading sponsors of global terrorism was Col. Muammar al-Qadaffi, the ruler of Libya. Using cash generated by his country's supply of oil, Qadaffi pur-

Reagan disliked Libyan leader Muammar al-Qadaffi because of Qadaffi's public criticism of the United States and support of anti-American causes.

chased weapons from the Soviets, supported anti-U.S. terrorists, and undermined efforts to promote peace between Arab nations and Israel in the Middle East.

Reagan called the Libyan leader "an unpredictable fanatic" and a "mad clown" who threatened stability in the Middle East. The insults that Qadaffi frequently directed at the United States affected Reagan on a personal level. "I tried to repress the hatred I felt for Qadaffi, but I couldn't do it," he later wrote in his autobiography.[43]

The question for the angry president was how to get Qadaffi under control. First, Reagan tried to intimidate him with a display of American military power. In 1981, he ordered U.S. warships to the Gulf of Sidra off Libya's northern coast, waters that Libya claimed as its own. Clashes between the two sides soon erupted, and Reagan was pleased when U.S. warplanes shot down two Libyan fighters over the gulf. "We'd sent Qadaffi a message," he later recalled.[44]

But the Libyan leader refused to back down. After Egyptian leader Anwar Sadat, who had won the Nobel Peace Prize for promoting peace between Arab nations and

Egyptian leader Anwar Sadat was killed by Muslim radicals in 1981. When Qadaffi celebrated his death, he gained the contempt not only of Reagan, but of most of the world.

Israel, was killed in 1981, Qadaffi celebrated his death on Libyan television. Sadat was murdered by Muslim radicals displeased by his efforts to bring about peace. In Paris and Rome, U.S. diplomats were threatened by various terrorist groups, and rumors of a Libyan plot against Reagan's life were taken seriously in Washington. Elsewhere in the world, the pace of terrorism increased. In July 1985, Muslim radicals hijacked an airplane with 153 passengers aboard, including 135 Americans. One American passenger was murdered, and the rest were released only after weeks of tense negotiations. In October, the Italian cruise ship *Achille Lauro* was hijacked by Palestinian terrorists, and again an American passenger was murdered.

STRIKING BACK AT TERRORISM

In his autobiography, Reagan writes of his decision to launch, in response to a terrorist attack, an air raid on the Libyan capital of Tripoli. The raid did not harm Libyan leader Muammar al-Qadaffi, but did kill or injure many Libyan citizens.

". . . I knew we had to do something about the crackpot in Tripoli. 'He's not only a barbarian, he's flaky,' I said at the time. I felt we had no alternative but a military response: As a matter of self-defense, any nation victimized by terrorism has an inherent right to respond with force to deter new acts of terror. I felt that we must show Qadaffi that there was a price he would have to pay for that kind of behavior, that we wouldn't let him get away with it. So I asked the Joint Chiefs of Staff for a plan. . . .

On April 13, we settled on a principal target: Qadaffi's military headquarters and barracks in Tripoli, which was located well away from civilian targets. Housed in this compound was the intelligence center from which Libya's worldwide program of state-sponsored terrorism was directed.

The attack was not intended to kill Qadaffi; that would have violated our prohibition against assassination. The objective was to let him know we weren't going to accept his terrorism anymore, and that if he did it again he could expect to hear from us again. It was impossible, however, to know exactly where he would be at the time of the attack. We realized that it was possible, perhaps probable, that he might be at or near the intelligence center when our planes struck."

Under growing pressure to act forcefully, the Reagan administration planned a military response for the next act of terrorism. In 1986, a Libyan-funded terrorist bombing in a Berlin discotheque killed two people and wounded 155 more, many of whom were American soldiers stationed in West Germany. Reagan ordered air strikes on the Libyan capital of Tripoli that killed civilians, including Qadaffi's infant daughter. The loss of civilian life was criticized by some of America's allies, but most Americans supported the president's decision to strike at terrorists where they lived. More importantly to Reagan, the air strikes put an end—for the time being, at least—to Qadaffi's anti-American activities.

THE MIDDLE EAST

Libya was far from the only source of trouble in the Middle East. The roots of terrorism and war in the region stretch back to the 1940s, when Israel was established as a Jewish nation in the midst of the Arab-dominated region. Decades of war and terrorism involving Israel and its Arab neighbors followed. The most troublesome issue was whether Palestine, a tiny Arab-occupied region on Israel's border, had the right to govern itself. Israel insisted that much of the Palestinians' land rightfully belonged to it, while the Arab nations in the region defended Palestine.

The issue of Palestinian independence, the main point of contention between Arab nations and Israel, was of less concern to Reagan and his advisors. The president's main fear was that the violence and instability in the region made it vulnerable to Soviet attempts to spread communism. As a result, Reagan offered few solutions to ending the violent struggle, and focused instead on developing what he called a "strategic consensus"—a coalition of Middle Eastern nations that were united against the Soviets.

Early in Reagan's first term, Secretary of State Alexander Haig traveled to Egypt, Israel, Jordan, and Saudi Arabia to warn them of the threat of Soviet invasion. Arab nations were unresponsive to Haig's warnings because they were more concerned about an Israeli attack. Saudi foreign minister Prince Saud made it clear that the Soviets were the least of his worries. "The Kingdom of Saudi Arabia regards Israel as the principal cause of instability and insecurity in the region," he said.[45]

Nor did the United States' attempts to strengthen its relations with Israel meet with much success. Reagan's decision to give sophisticated military aircraft to Saudi Arabia angered Israeli leader Menachem Begin, who saw the planes as a threat to his country's national security.

The October 1981 assassination of Egyptian president Anwar Sadat, a leading advocate of peace between Israel and its Arab neighbors, added to the tension. In the summer of 1982, the Israeli army drove the Palestinians out of their position in the West Bank region, and invaded the small nation of Lebanon in pursuit of fleeing Arab forces. The situation in the Middle East threatened to explode.

Secretary of State Alexander Haig traveled to Egypt, Israel, Jordan, and Saudi Arabia in the beginning of Reagan's presidency.

TRAGEDY IN LEBANON

After seeing video footage of Lebanese civilians injured by Israeli bombs, Reagan finally asked Begin to call off the attack. In September of 1982, Reagan offered a peace plan for the region that would set aside a homeland for the 1.3 million displaced Palestinians, in return for the Arab world's recognition of Israel's right to exist. Neither side endorsed all the specifics of the plan, but they did agree to a cease-fire. The United States, France, and Italy moved troops into Beirut to enforce the fragile truce.

Instead of bringing calm to Lebanon, the peacekeeping force quickly found itself under attack. Radical Muslims who opposed the idea of peace with Israel began a campaign of violence designed to drive the foreign troops out. In April of 1983, a terrorist attack killed sixty-three people at the U.S. embassy in Beirut. Six months later, on October 23, terrorists drove a truck filled with twelve thousand pounds of explosives into the U.S. Marine barracks in Beirut, killing 241 Marines. A nearby bombing killed fifty-eight French soldiers.

In a televised speech, Reagan praised the bravery of the soldiers who were killed and vowed that the act of terrorism would not drive the United States out of Lebanon. Once again, he emphasized the region's strategic importance in the global battle against communism:

> If terrorism and intimidation succeed, it'll be a devastating blow to the peace process and to Israel's search for genuine security. It won't just be Lebanon sentenced to a future of chaos. Can the United States, or the free world for that matter, stand by and see the Middle East incorporated into the Soviet bloc?[46]

But the American people were haunted by memories of the Vietnam War. More than fifty-eight thousand American soldiers died in Vietnam before the U.S. government finally admitted defeat in 1973. The most difficult part of the war for many Americans was that they could not understand why it was fought in the first place.

No one wanted to let a similar tragedy occur in the Middle East. Ernest Hollings, a senator from South Carolina, said of the troops that gave their lives in Lebanon: "They do not have a mission. If they were put there to fight, there are too few. If they were put there to die, there are too many."[47] An editorial in the national newspaper *USA Today* echoed Hollings's concern: "Through our tears and anger, many Americans will be asking again the punishing question: Why are our fighting men in Lebanon?"[48]

In his 1984 State of the Union address, Reagan argued one last time for a continued U.S. military presence in Lebanon. Two weeks later, under intense pressure from Congress and the public, he ordered the troops out.

THE INVASION OF GRENADA

Just days after the tragedy in Lebanon, Reagan had another reason to send the American military into action. This time, the mission was far more successful.

The island nation of Grenada is a former British colony located in the Caribbean Sea. In 1979, a Communist government seized control of the tiny island nation and opened relations with Cuba, Nicaragua,

Emergency crews work in the rubble of the U.S. Marine barracks after a terrorist bomb destroyed the building, killing 241 servicemen.

and the Soviet Union. With help from the Cuban government, the communists began to build an airport that they claimed would help their tourism industry.

Reagan worried that the new airport could be used to launch attacks against the United States. He was also concerned about the safety of the eight hundred American medical students who lived in Grenada. Six former British colonies in the Caribbean formally requested that the United States restore order in Grenada, adding to Reagan's worries. When an even more extreme government took over and imposed martial law, Reagan decided to take action. On October 25, 1983—two days after the bombing in Lebanon—he ordered the U.S. Marines and Army to invade the island. The battle was over quickly. The U.S. troops overwhelmed the small, lightly armed band of Cubans and Grenadans in a few days.

REAGAN EXPLAINS THE GRENADA INVASION

In an October 27, 1983 address to the nation, Reagan explained how the death of 241 U.S. Marines in Lebanon was related to the American invasion of Grenada just days later.

"The events in Lebanon and Grenada, though oceans apart, are closely related. Not only has Moscow assisted and encouraged the violence in both countries, but it provides direct support through a network of surrogates and terrorists. It is no coincidence that when the thugs tried to wrest control over Grenada, there were thirty Soviet advisers and hundreds of Cuban military and paramilitary forces on the island. . . .

. . . You know, there was a time when our national security was based on a standing army here within our own borders and shore batteries of artillery along our coasts, and of course, a navy to keep the sea-lanes open for the shipping of things necessary to our well-being. The world has changed. Today, our national security can be threatened in faraway places. It's up to all of us to be aware of the strategic importance of such places and to be able to identify them.

Sam Rayburn once said that freedom is not something a nation can work for once and win forever. He said it's like an insurance policy; its premiums must be kept up to date. In order to keep it, we have to keep working for it and sacrificing for it just as long as we live. If we do not, our children may not know the pleasure of working to keep it, for it may not be theirs to keep."

Although 19 Americans were killed and 115 more wounded, the invasion was a success and came at just the right time for a nation reeling from the tragedy in the Middle East. The nightly news programs were filled with images of returning medical students falling to their knees and kissing American soil. Reagan heaped praise on the troops, showering them with some eight thousand medals and reporting that the United States had captured enough Cuban weapons to supply an army of terrorists.

In a televised speech on October 27, 1983, Reagan made the connection between two recent events that took place thousands of miles apart:

> The events in Lebanon and Grenada, though oceans apart, are closely related. Not only has Moscow assisted and encouraged the violence in both countries, but it provides direct support through a network of surrogates and terrorists. It is no coincidence that when the thugs tried to wrest control over Grenada, there were thirty Soviet advisers and hundreds of Cuban military and paramilitary forces on the island.[49]

From Reagan's perspective, the invasion of tiny Grenada was a triumph in the larger battle to stop the spread of communism.

SEEKING ALLIES

While Reagan was struggling to control state-sponsored terrorism and establish order in the Middle East, he was also seeking new allies in the struggle against the Soviet Union. And no country had bigger potential as an ally than the People's Republic of China. Although it had a Communist government, the nation of some one billion people was not a Soviet ally. China also boasted a powerful military and a strategic location right on the Soviet border, two factors that could help tip the balance of power in the Cold War in the West's favor.

Reagan made improved relations with China a top priority, just as it had been for presidents Nixon, Ford, and Carter. To strengthen ties early in his first term, the president invited the Chinese government to buy American military equipment. He was convinced that China could be made a part of the United States' larger anti-Soviet efforts.

Reagan nearly drove the Chinese government to the Soviet side, however, by also offering to sell weapons to the anticommunist government of Taiwan, a small island off the coast of mainland China. China saw the arms sales as a threat to its national security. When Reagan refused to change his decision, China showed interest in improving relations with the Soviet Union, and became harshly critical of U.S. actions in the Middle East and Central America.

Later in his presidency, Reagan was able to establish a stronger relationship with the Chinese. In 1984, the Chinese prime minister became the first Communist leader of his country to visit the United States. Several months later, Reagan visited China, the first time he had ever set foot in a Communist country. After he agreed to limit the amount of U.S. aid to Taiwan, he and Chinese leaders took steps toward improved trade and economic cooperation.

Seeking Support in Europe

Reagan had a ready-made group of allies in the members of the North Atlantic Treaty Organization (NATO), a military alliance formed in 1949 to present a united front of opposition to the Soviet Union and its Eastern European allies.

While America was thousands of miles away from the Soviet Union, the Western European countries that formed the core

---

Sending the Soviets a Message

In his autobiography, the president explains the strategy of containment of communism that guided his foreign policy.

"As the foundation of my foreign policy, I decided we had to send as powerful a message as we could to the Russians that we weren't going to stand by anymore while they armed and financed terrorists and subverted democratic governments. Our policy was to be one based on strength and realism. I wanted peace through strength, not peace through a piece of paper.

In my speeches and press conferences, I deliberately set out to say some frank things about the Russians, to let them know there were some new fellows in Washington who had a realistic view of what they were up to and weren't going to let them keep it up. At my first press conference I was asked whether we could trust the Soviet Union, and I said that the answer to that question could be found in the writings of Soviet leaders: It had always been their philosophy that it was moral to lie or cheat for the purpose of advancing Communism. I said they had told us, without meaning to, that they couldn't be trusted. . . .

I wanted to let them know that in attempting to continue their policy of expansionism, they were prolonging the nuclear arms race and keeping the world on the precipice of disaster. I also wanted to send the signal that we weren't going to be deceived by words into thinking they'd changed their stripes: We wanted deeds, not words. And I intended to let them know that we were going to spend whatever it took to stay ahead of them in the arms race. We would never accept second place."

of NATO shared borders with Communist countries. With Soviet missiles so close, they feared that they would be the first to die in a nuclear war—a belief that made a Soviet-U.S. arms control agreement vitally important to them. Many found Reagan's harsh anti-Soviet talk and massive arms buildup alarming. They feared that the American leader could push the world into a war in which their continent, and not North America, would be the battleground.

Reagan made six visits to his NATO allies in Europe over the course of his presidency. The trips, according to a 1982 article in the *Wall Street Journal,* had a simple purpose: "To convince ordinary European men and women that Mr. Reagan is a sensible and reliable ally rather than the simple-minded, trigger-happy cowboy that many of them still consider him to be."[50]

Reagan's first trip to Europe, in June of 1982, took him through France, the Vatican, Italy, Britain, and West Germany. As he always did for trips abroad, he prepared carefully by watching training films that included images of where he was going and who he would meet.

He spoke convincingly to the British Parliament of his commitment to arms control negotiations with the Soviets. Before Germany's political leaders, he emphasized his willingness to reduce the size of America's nuclear arsenal. The effect of the visit was enough to convince many Europeans that the American president would not lead the NATO alliance into war.

READY FOR REELECTION

There were signs of trouble for Reagan in 1984, as he prepared to seek reelection. Terrorists threatened Americans abroad, arms negotiations with the Soviets were stalled, and the budget deficit had grown by billions of dollars.

But Reagan always rose to the challenge of a campaign, and his June 1984 appearance in Normandy, France, served as a warning to his opponents that he had not lost his political gifts. In a speech marking the fortieth anniversary of the Allied invasion of Europe, he honored the American soldiers who had risked their lives to capture the cliffs:

> Behind me is a memorial that symbolizes the Ranger daggers that were thrust into the tops of these cliffs. And before me are the men who put them there. These are the boys of Pointe du Hoc. These are the men who took the cliffs. These are the champions who helped free a continent. These are the heroes who helped end a war.[51]

The American soldiers in the audience were moved to tears, as were members of the press. Reagan still had the ability to tap America's deepest feelings of patriotism and pride. He was ready for the campaign trail.

5 Four More Years

As Reagan began his bid for a second term in office in 1984, one thing was abundantly clear: Nothing that went wrong during his first term in office—not an enormous federal deficit, or continued hostilities with the Soviets, or the death of 241 Marines in Lebanon—had any lasting effect on the public's support for him. He was, as Democratic congresswoman Pat Schroeder of Colorado called him, the "Teflon President."[52]

Reagan's popularity was so great that he did not feel any pressure to offer voters new ideas during his reelection campaign.

In 1984 Reagan was a popular choice for reelection.

Walter Mondale, Reagan's Democratic opponent in 1984, had the first female running mate in history. Mondale attacked both Reagan's policies and his age.

Instead, he fell back on the plans and proposals that had won him the presidency four years earlier. He again reached out to the most conservative Americans, the New Right, with a call for a constitutional amendment to ban abortion. He echoed his 1980 accusations that the Democrats were the party of high taxes and inflation and warned that a vote for them would throw the country right back in the economic mess it had suffered through in the 1970s.

His Democratic opponent was Walter Mondale, former vice president under Jimmy Carter. Mondale announced a detailed campaign platform, including opposition to building the Star Wars defense system, the MX missile, and the B-1 bomber. He also announced his support for a freeze on nuclear weapons spending. He advocated higher taxes on corporations and the wealthy to address record deficits. And, in a historic move, he announced that Geraldine Ferraro would be

his running mate, the first time in history a woman was selected as a major-party candidate for vice president.

While Mondale delved into specifics, trying to convince Americans that the economic situation was not as bright as Reagan would have them believe, Reagan avoided confrontation with his opponent and continued his campaign aimed at tapping into the country's sense of pride. "The United States of America was never meant to be a second-rate nation," the president said. "So, like our Olympic athletes, let's aim for the stars and go for the gold. . . . America's best days are yet to come."[53]

The text from one of Reagan's television advertisements perfectly captures the upbeat tone of his 1984 campaign:

> It's morning again in America. Today, more men and women will go to work than ever before in our country's history. With interest rates at about half the record high of 1980, nearly two

thousand families today will buy new homes, more than at any time in the past four years. This afternoon, sixty-five hundred young men and women will be married, and with inflation at less than half of what it was four years ago, they can look forward with confidence. It's morning again in America. And under the leadership of President Reagan, our country is stronger, and prouder, and better. Why would we ever want to return to where we were less than four short years ago?[54]

Chinks in his political armor were visible only once during the campaign. In the first debate between the candidates, Reagan misquoted statistics, appeared confused at times, and stumbled badly over his words in his closing remarks. Democrats were quick to attribute the mistakes to Reagan's age; he was seventy-three at the time.

But to his advisors, Reagan's mistake was that he had simply failed to prepare properly for the debate. Campaign consultant Stuart Spencer downplayed the age factor, saying, "The bottom line is that Ronald Reagan didn't do his homework; he got lazy . . . he was given his briefing books. He took them up to Camp David, and they sat over there, and he was watching old movies."[55]

Reagan put his campaign back on track at the second debate in Kansas City. Before some 100 million viewers, he answered a question about his age with one of the most memorable lines of his presidency: "I'm not going to exploit for political purposes my opponent's youth and inexperience."[56]

The line was a hit with American voters, as was Reagan's campaign. He aroused the public's pride when he announced in one speech that "America is back, standing tall, looking to the eighties with courage, confidence, and hope."[57] Buoyed by his personal charm, political skill, and a rebounding economy, he went on to win the election in a landslide. He captured 59 percent of the votes and won every state except Mondale's native Minnesota.

Reagan's election victory was so convincing that even his fiercest political opponents were impressed. "In my fifty years of public life," Speaker of the House Tip O'Neill told Reagan, "I've never seen a man more popular than you with the American people."[58] Meanwhile, Mondale could only ponder why he had lost. "I tried to get specific and Reagan patted dogs," he later said about the 1984 campaign. "I should have patted more dogs."[59]

MORNING AGAIN IN AMERICA?

Reagan's 1984 campaign ads had proclaimed with optimism that it was "morning again in America." For most Americans, this seemed to be the case—four out of five surveyed said that they were better off economically than they were before Reagan's first term.

But the millions of poor Americans had not fared as well. In the fight to fix the economy during his first term, the Reagan administration had slashed social programs, including Medicaid, food stamps, child nutrition programs, low-income housing and energy assistance, and unemployment insurance.

According to a study of his first term by a private research organization, the Urban Institute, the household income for the poorest 20 percent actually dropped 8 percent to just $6,391. The same study found that for the richest 20 percent of Americans, average family income rose 9 percent to $40,888.

BREAKING UP THE TROIKA

As Reagan's second term began, he started to lose his most trusted advisors. Some, like longtime aide Lyn Nofziger, grew weary of the long hours and low pay of public office, and went off to seek their fortunes in private life. Others were forced out by allegations that they had violated ethical or legal standards. Secretary of Labor Raymond Donovan, for example, was forced to resign in the face of charges that he had cheated the New York Transit Authority out of more than 7 million dollars.

Soon after his reelection, Reagan also lost the "troika"—the three staff members who were crucial to the successes of his first term. Ed Meese, Michael Deaver, and

During Reagan's second term he lost valuable staff members James Baker, Ed Meese, and Michael Deaver (left to right).

James Baker had borne responsibility for most of the day-to-day affairs of government, including staff management and bringing policy recommendations to Reagan for his approval.

Deaver, the mastermind of the president's public image, resigned in 1985 to become a Washington lobbyist, hired by corporations to influence government decisions about industry rules and regulations. Meese's seven and one-half years in the Reagan administration, first as counsellor and then as attorney general, were marked by repeated investigations into his financial and ethical conduct. And Chief of Staff James Baker, a master of the ins and outs of Washington politics, grew weary of his stressful position. With Reagan's approval, he and Secretary of the Treasury Donald Regan swapped jobs in January of 1985.

Though the three men had rarely agreed on anything, each had been very loyal to the president. They had worked effectively together to accomplish his goals and, as much as possible, protect him from missteps.

Dealing with the departure of trusted staff members was difficult for a president who depended so heavily on them to make key decisions. Reagan's habit of delegating authority whenever possible started during his days as governor of California. "He really did believe that you hired people you trust," remembered White House spokesman, Larry Speakes, "and then you let them do their job."[60]

This trend continued in the White House. Reagan preferred not to get bogged down in the details of any particular issue and had little interest in briefing books and complex discussions. "Ronald Reagan is not a stupid person, but he was the least curious person I ever met," commented one member of his administration.[61] To prepare him for meetings, his staff would write out talking points for him on index cards; the president would often read directly from the cards, even in one-on-one meetings.

The president's willingness to delegate authority led some members of his administration to wonder who, if anyone, was really in charge. Alexander Haig, Reagan's first secretary of state, wrote in his memoirs:

> To me, the White House was as mysterious as a ghost ship; you heard the creak of the rigging and the groan of the timbers, and sometimes even glimpsed the crew on deck. But which of the crew had the helm? . . . It was impossible to tell.[62]

Reagan himself was so confident in his staff's abilities that he allowed himself frequent vacations to the presidential retreat in Maryland and to his home state of California, where he would spend a combined total of 345 days out of his eight-year presidency.

STAYING THE COURSE

While Reagan's advisors changed, the issues and policies varied little from the first term to the second. According to campaign manager Ed Rollins, even after the 1984 election the administration still lacked a

Pressuring the Soviet Economy

As Reagan explains in the following passage from his autobiography, he long believed that American capitalism and democracy would triumph over Soviet communism in the Cold War. And he believed that forcing the Soviets to match U.S. military spending would drive their economy into deeper trouble.

"I learned the Soviet economy was in even worse shape than I'd realized. I had always believed that, as an economic system, Communism was doomed. Not only was it lacking in the free market incentives that motivated people to work hard and excel—the economic propulsion that had brought such prosperity to America—but history was full of examples showing that any totalitarian state that deprived its people of liberty and freedom of choice was ultimately doomed. The Bolshevik Revolution had simply replaced an inherited aristocracy with a self-appointed one, the Soviet leadership, and it, like its predecessor, could not survive against the inherent drive of all men and women to be free.

Now, the economic statistics and intelligence reports I was getting during my daily National Security Council briefings were revealing tangible evidence that Communism as we knew it was approaching the brink of collapse, not only in the Soviet Union but throughout the Eastern bloc. The Soviet economy was being held together with baling wire; it was a basket case, partly because of massive spending on armaments. . . .

You had to wonder how long the Soviets could keep their empire intact. If they didn't make some changes, it seemed clear to me that in time Communism would collapse of its own weight, and I wondered how we as a nation could use these cracks in the Soviet system to accelerate the process of collapse."

plan for the next four years in office. "We'd run an issueless campaign," said Rollins. "There was no second-term plan. During the time they should have been thinking one up, the White House was completely paralyzed."[63] The majority of Americans approved of Reagan's first-term performance, the Reagan administration reasoned, so why try anything new?

Adding to the complacency was the feeling that Reagan had already accomplished what he had set out to do in 1980. Tax rates had been cut, many government programs had been eliminated or reduced, and the nation's military might had been restored.

The economy, troubled even during Reagan's first two years in office, had recovered nicely. A record number of Americans were now employed, and the rate of inflation that had once rocketed to 12 percent had dropped to just 3.7 percent.

The biggest exception to this bright economic picture was the huge federal deficit. Although this issue would occupy Reagan and Congress for most of 1985, the president was reluctant to try new solutions.

Reagan's first move in 1985, just as it had been in 1981, was to trim spending on federal programs. But this time around, Congress rejected his proposal to chop $60 billion off the budget. Instead, they decided on a more drastic measure; for the first time since 1975, they reduced the amount of defense spending.

One of the few new domestic initiatives that Reagan undertook in his second term was focused on the familiar goal of lower taxes. In May of 1985, he introduced a plan for tax reform that would shift some of the burden from individuals to corporations and simplify the existing tax system. After a bitter political battle, Congress passed the Tax Reform Act in 1986. It cut the maximum tax rate for individuals from 50 to 28 percent and eliminated loopholes that allowed people to avoid paying taxes.

MEETING WITH GORBACHEV

While Reagan stayed on a familiar course at home early in his second term, changes were taking place in the Soviet Union that set the stage for his biggest foreign policy achievement—the end of the nuclear arms race.

In the two years since the Geneva arms control talks broke up, U.S.-Soviet relations had not improved. Two Soviet leaders, Yuri Andropov and Konstantin Chernenko, had died in quick succession, leaving behind a shaky government and an even shakier economy. Meanwhile, Reagan continued his tough anti-Soviet talk and pumped billions more dollars into nuclear weapons development.

When Mikhail Gorbachev came to power in 1985, Reagan greeted him with the wariness he typically had for Soviet leaders. "There's a great mutual suspicion between the two countries," he said in response to Gorbachev's election. "I think ours is more justified than theirs."[64]

But Gorbachev was a different kind of Soviet leader. At fifty-four years of age, he was the youngest man to lead the Soviet Union in fifty years. He was energetic and ambitious, unlike the two sickly leaders before him. He cracked down on government corruption, and announced his intention of curing his country's ills through better leadership and more disciplined government spending.

Gorbachev also had a program for domestic reform called perestroika (restructuring) that was intended to reverse the nation's two-decade-long economic slide. While the Soviet Union in 1984 remained a giant producer of steel, cement, machinery, and other industrial goods, the world economy had changed dramatically. The information age was dawning, and computers

GORBACHEV REACHES OUT TO REAGAN

Soon after taking office, Soviet General Secretary Mikhail Gorbachev sent Reagan a personal letter, the tone of which was an early sign of the improved U.S.-U.S.S.R. relations that would lead to a nuclear arms control agreement. The letter is quoted in Reagan's autobiography, An American Life.

"Our countries are different by their social systems, by the ideologies dominant in them—but we believe that this should not be a reason for animosity. Each social system has the right to life, and it should prove its advantages not by force, not by military means, but on the path of peaceful competition with the other system. And all people have the right to go the way they have chosen themselves, without anybody imposing his will on them from outside, interfering in their internal affairs. We believe that this is the only just and healthy basis for relations among states. For our part, we have always striven to build our relations with the United States, as well as with other countries, precisely in this manner. . . . I am convinced that given such an approach to the business at hand, on the basis of a reasonable account of the realities of today's world and treating with a due respect the rights and legitimate interests of the other side, we could do quite a bit to benefit the peoples of our countries, as well as the whole world having embarked on the road of a real improvement of relations."

and electronics, rather than heavy machinery, were essential to a thriving economy.

Gorbachev was quick to realize that he could not make the transition from an industry-based economy to a technology-based economy while so much of the country's resources were devoted to matching the United States in the nuclear arms race. For him, ending the arms race was essential to reviving the slumping Soviet economy.

Witty, warm, and dynamic, Gorbachev quickly charmed the Western public. He gave interviews to *Time* magazine and French journalists, something his predecessors never did, and he heralded the arrival of glasnost, or the spirit of openness— a series of reforms intended to give Soviet citizens greater political, intellectual, and religious freedoms. It was clear that a new era had begun. Gorbachev was ready to move beyond the Cold War, and he wanted to develop a positive relationship with the U.S. president.

In his public statements, Reagan showed that he, too, was ready for a new beginning.

Early in Reagan's second term he was able to improve relations with the Soviet Union's new leader, Mikhail Gorbachev, who was willing to negotiate with the United States.

The U.S. military buildup that he directed during his first term made him confident that he could now negotiate with the Soviets from a position of strength. As he prepared to open arms reduction talks, the hostile language he once used to describe the Soviet Union faded away. He no longer made references to "the evil empire" as he had in a 1983 speech, and he avoided repeating his earlier description of U.S.-Soviet relations as a "struggle between right and wrong and good and evil."[65] Instead, Reagan began to refer to the Cold War in more moderate terms, as a misunderstanding between the two nations that could be repaired through negotiation.

While the president was suspicious of Gorbachev's intentions at first, he gradually came to view him as someone he could do business with. In an April 4, 1985, letter to Gorbachev, he indicated his own willingness to improve relations between the two countries. "I believe that new opportunities are now opening up in U.S.-Soviet relations," he wrote. "We must take advantage of them."[66]

MORE TALKS IN GENEVA

Renewed arms negotiations in Geneva were a sign that both sides recognized the time was ripe for a new type of diplomacy. However, the road to an actual arms control agreement was rough. A one-on-one meeting between the two leaders in Geneva, Switzerland, in November of 1985 produced nothing more than an agreement that the two leaders would meet again.

One of the biggest obstacles to reaching an agreement was Reagan's refusal to back away from the Strategic Defense Initiative (SDI). Reagan had decided even before negotiations began that he would not trade away SDI for the Soviet promise to reduce nuclear weapons. But to Gorbachev, SDI was a military threat because, although it was still far from being a reality, it could give the United States immunity from Soviet missiles. At the same time, Gorbachev believed that he would be forced to spend billions to build a defensive shield of his own.

The United States was, in turn, concerned over Gorbachev's refusal to permit on-site

THE GENEVA SUMMIT

In the following passage from his autobiography, Reagan describes his first meeting with the new Soviet leader, Mikhail Gorbachev, at the 1985 arms control talks in Geneva. At the meeting, Reagan and Gorbachev began a personal relationship that would later lead to a nuclear arms control agreement.

"Usually at summit conferences, the real work is done in advance by diplomats and specialists on each side who, based on guidance from their superiors, do the spadework and work out any agreements that are to be signed at the meeting, after which the top leaders come in and preside over the formalities.

Starting with Brezhnev, I'd dreamed of personally going one-on-one with a Soviet leader because I thought we might be able to accomplish things our countries' diplomats couldn't do because they didn't have the authority. Putting that another way, I felt if you got the top people negotiating and talking at a summit and then the two of you came out arm in arm saying, 'We've agreed to this,' the bureaucrats wouldn't be able to louse up the agreement. Until Gorbachev, I never got the opportunity to try out my idea. Now I had my chance. . . .

As we shook hands for the first time, I had to admit—as Margaret Thatcher and Prime Minister Brian Mulroney of Canada predicted I would—that there was something likable about Gorbachev. There was warmth in his face and his style, not the coldness bordering on hatred I'd seen in most senior Soviet officials I'd met until then. . . .

As we flew home I felt good: Gorbachev was tough and convinced Communism was superior to capitalism, but after almost five years I'd finally met a Soviet leader I could talk to."

inspections to ensure compliance with any arms control agreement that was signed. They also wanted a withdrawal of Soviet forces from Afghanistan. At a second meeting in Iceland almost a year later, the talks again broke up over these two issues.

Reagan left the 1986 Iceland meeting in a grim state of mind, and his secretary of state, George Shultz, appeared dejected before the international media. *Time* magazine's cover that week announced the end of talks and blamed the United States—"No Deal: Star Wars sinks the Summit."[67] An arms control agreement once again seemed a distant dream.

But the two leaders had developed a personal relationship that would move the peace process forward in spite of their deep disagreements. Gorbachev realized that even the United States could barely support the cost of a proposed SDI system; if he were to offer an appealing missile reduction proposal, the United States might kill the SDI program on its own.

THE INF TREATY

Gorbachev met with Reagan in Washington on December 8, 1987. The American people showed their desire for peace by welcoming the Soviet leader with open arms. Gorbachev was charming as ever, winning the respect of members of Congress, celebrities, and the public.

Late in 1987, Gorbachev and Reagan signed the Intermediate Nuclear Forces Treaty, which began the process of dismantling nuclear weapons in both countries.

The Intermediate Nuclear Forces Treaty (INF) that the two leaders signed in Washington was a historic step. For the first time, a whole class of nuclear weapons was eliminated. Gorbachev made the treaty possible by dropping his demands that the SDI program be eliminated and agreeing to a plan for on-site inspections.

Under the terms of the treaty, 859 U.S. and 1,836 Soviet missiles would be destroyed over three years. This amounted to just 4 percent of the total nuclear arsenals of the two sides, which still had some 30,000 nuclear weapons aimed at each other. The deal was criticized by conservatives, including Reagan's own chief arms negotiator, because it eliminated U.S. missiles in Western Europe that could reach the Soviet Union in just minutes. But the American public was relieved by the prospect of peace. Four in five Americans supported the INF treaty, according to one poll.

Perhaps most surprising of all was that the agreement came at the direction of Reagan, a president who once promised to be tougher on the Soviet Union than any of his predecessors. Even Gorbachev was amazed. "Who would have thought in the early eighties," Gorbachev wondered, "that it would be Ronald Reagan who would sign with us the first nuclear-arms reduction agreement in history?"[68]

In 1988, Reagan set foot on Soviet soil for the first time. In a speech set in front of a giant bust of Lenin, the president attempted to, he said later, "explain America and what we are all about":

> Political leadership in a democracy requires seeing past the abstractions and embracing the vast diversity of humanity, and doing it with humility; listening as best you can, not just to those in high positions, but to the cacophonous voices of ordinary people, and trusting those millions of people, keeping out of their way. . . . And the word we have for this is "freedom."[69]

Ten years earlier, it would have been an unthinkable scene: crowds of Soviet people cheering an American president as he praised democracy and the American way. But a new era had begun with the long-awaited arms control agreement, and the Cold War had drawn to a close.

6 The Iran-Contra Affair

Not all of Reagan's foreign policy ventures were as successful as his arms control agreement with the Soviets. With the exception of communism, nothing troubled the president more than the issue of Americans taken hostage by terrorists abroad. He remembered vividly how he had used the hostage situation against Carter during the 1980 campaign, when he had insisted that he would never negotiate with Iranian or any other terrorists. He did not want to be remembered as a weak president who was unable to protect Americans abroad, but during Reagan's tenure as president, a number of Americans were being held against their will in foreign countries. Reagan's chief of staff Donald Regan described the president's concern for hostages:

> He's got the same situation [as Carter did], and he's responsible for it and he's thinking to himself, 'What's history going to say about me?' And here are these poor people in jail, being browbeaten, tortured. . . . Ronald Reagan eats his heart out over this. It worries him. It's with him.[70]

Reagan's second term was marked by his struggle to deal with the twin issues of communism and hostages. They came together in what became known as the Iran-contra affair.

THE COMMUNIST THREAT IN CENTRAL AMERICA

The story of the Iran-contra affair begins in Nicaragua, a small, poverty-stricken Central American nation. In 1979, Nicaraguan dictator Anastasio Somoza was driven from power, and Daniel Ortega, the leader of a band of rebels called the Sandanistas, seized control of the government. Ortega quickly established ties to the Soviet Union and Cuba and began to receive military and economic aid from the two communist nations.

The events in Nicaragua worried Reagan and his staff. They feared that the existence of a strong communist government in Nicaragua might set off a "domino effect" throughout Central America, in which one country after another could fall under communist control. To justify these fears, Reagan pointed out that Ortega was already allowing Soviet and Cuban weapons to flow through Nicaragua to communist rebels trying to overthrow the

FIGHTING COMMUNISM IN CENTRAL AMERICA

In an April 27, 1983 address, quoted in Speaking My Mind, *Reagan urged a joint session of Congress to support aid to contras and other Central American countries. He argued that the aid was necessary to remove the threat of a Soviet presence so close to America.*

"El Salvador is nearer to Texas than Texas is to Massachusetts. Nicaragua is just as close to Miami, San Antonio, San Diego, and Tucson as those cities are to Washington, where we're gathered tonight.

But nearness on the map doesn't even begin to tell the strategic importance of Central America, bordering as it does on the Caribbean—our lifeline to the outside world. . . . If the Nazis during World War II and the Soviets today recognize the Caribbean and Central America as vital to our interests, shouldn't we, also? For several years now, under two administrations, the United States has been increasing its defense of freedom in the Caribbean basin. And I can tell you tonight, democracy is beginning to take root in El Salvador, which, until a short time ago, knew only dictatorship.

The new government is now delivering on its promises of democracy, reforms, and free elections. It wasn't easy, and there was resistance to many of the attempted reforms, with assassinations of some of the reformers. Guerrilla bands and urban terrorists were portrayed in a worldwide propaganda campaign as freedom fighters, representative of the people. Ten days before I came into office, the guerrillas launched what they called 'a final offensive' to overthrow the government. And their radio boasted that our new administration would be too late to prevent their victory. Well, they learned that democracy cannot be so easily defeated. . . .

Yes, there are still major problems regarding human rights, the criminal justice system, and violence against noncombatants. And like the rest of Central America, El Salvador also faces severe economic problems. . . . But as the previous election showed, the Salvadoran people's desire for democracy will not be defeated."

U.S.-backed government in neighboring El Salvador.

Reagan, who had so often stated his intention of halting the spread of communism in faraway places such as the Middle East, was equally determined to fight the spread of communism so close to the United States. In March of 1981, motivated by the belief that the government of Nicaragua posed a threat to national security, Reagan authorized $20 million in U.S. aid to build a small group of rebels called the contras into a fighting force capable of toppling the Sandanista government.

At first, aid to the contras was a closely held secret. Administration officials informed only the handful of congressional leaders who were required by law to approve all covert aid. There were two reasons for the secrecy. First, many members of Congress disagreed with Reagan's assessment of the threat posed by the Sandanista government. While conservative Republicans believed that the Sandanistas were committed communists intent on causing disorder at America's doorstep, many Democrats believed that the Sandanistas were simply a young government in the early stages of political reforms. The Democrats believed that economic aid could be used to encourage democratic reforms within Nicaragua and halt the export of arms to El Salvador.

The second reason for secrecy was that Reagan and his advisors feared the American public would not support his use of military aid to contain communism in Nicaragua. The U.S. involvement in Vietnam began quietly in the 1960s with the commitment of military aid and advisors

to an anticommunist South Vietnamese government; it had ended in an unpopular war that cost some fifty-eight thousand American lives. The American public was determined to avoid another conflict in which U.S. troops were drawn gradually into a costly war.

Aid to the contras would not remain under wraps for long, however. In 1982, the press uncovered Reagan's early aid to the contras and reported that thousands of innocent civilians had been killed by rebel forces. Congress moved quickly to halt Reagan's secret efforts to topple the Sandanista government, passing the Boland Amendment by a vote of 411 to 0. The legislation barred any covert aid that was intended "for the purpose of overthrowing the government of Nicaragua."[71]

Reagan's advisors quickly found a loophole in the Boland Amendment. The director of the Central Intelligence Agency (CIA), William Casey, convinced members of Congress that covert aid to the contras was not being used to overthrow the Sandanista government, but instead to give them enough support so that their demands for peaceful democratic reform would be heeded by the Sandanistas.

While the secret aid continued, Reagan made a public plea for the contra cause during a May 9, 1984, television address.

> The Sandanista rule is a Communist reign of terror. Many of those who fought alongside the Sandanistas saw their revolution betrayed. They were denied power in the new government. Some were imprisoned, others exiled. Thousands who fought with the Sandanistas have taken up arms

Lieutenant Colonel Oliver North testifies at the Iran-contra hearings. North was instrumental in finding contributors to support the contras after Congress prohibited support of the rebels.

against them and are now called the contras. They are freedom fighters.[72]

The Reagan administration's efforts to circumvent congressional restrictions on aid to the contras were uncovered in 1984, when the *Wall Street Journal* reported that the CIA had secretly placed mines in Nicaraguan harbors to aid contra military efforts. It was also reported that a CIA training manual of assassination and sabotage techniques had been distributed to contra soldiers. In August of 1984, Congress passed a tougher version of the Boland Amendment, with the intention of preventing the CIA and the Defense Department from aiding the rebels in any way. Congressman Edward Boland of Massachusetts, the author of the bill, called the prohibition "airtight with no exceptions."[73] He added that the bill "clearly ends U.S. support for the war in Nicaragua."[74]

Boland believed that his law halted Reagan's support for the contras once and for all—but he was mistaken. In 1985, Reagan told his national security advisor, Robert McFarlane, "I want you to do whatever you have to do to help these people [the contras] keep body and soul together."[75] McFarlane and his assistant, a Marine lieutenant colonel named Oliver North, intensified their efforts to find private donors to support the contras. Saudi Arabia, which at McFarlane's request had secretly started to support the contras in 1984, upped its contribution to $2 million a month. Meanwhile, North met with potential contributors in the United States, and directed weapons, supplies, and money to the contras despite the ban on such aid put in place by the second Boland Amendment.

WEAPONS FOR HOSTAGES

As the U.S. involvement with the contras escalated, the other piece to the Iran-contra puzzle was taking shape thousands of miles away in the Middle East. Iran had once been an ally of the United States, but that changed in 1979 when the Ayatollah Khomeini and his supporters overthrew the government. Iranian radicals took fifty-two Americans hostage in the Iranian capital of Tehran, and the relations between the two countries soured.

Arms shipments to Iran were suspended in 1979 as part of President Carter's efforts to get the hostages home safely. And although the fifty-two hostages were returned safely on the day Reagan took office, the new president went even further. In 1983, he launched Operation Staunch, a program to stop other nations from selling Iran the weapons it needed for its war with neighboring Iraq.

The president and many others also believed that Iran was behind terrorist acts against the United States, including the 1983 bombing of the Marine barracks in Lebanon—and he vowed that he would have nothing to do with terrorists. "The United States gives terrorists no rewards and no guarantees," he stated firmly in 1985. "We make no concessions; we make no deals."[76] A year later, he signed a law prohibiting all military sales to nations, including Iran, that supported terrorism.

In spite of Operation Staunch and his own public statements, Reagan agreed to sell arms to Iran in 1985. Reagan gave military aid to an acknowledged enemy for one main reason; he believed that Iran could help him gain the release of seven American hostages who were being held in Lebanon at the time by a terrorist group with Iranian ties.

While he maintained a tough public stance of refusing to negotiate with terrorists who held U.S. citizens captive, he was willing to bend this policy to get them back. As he wrote in his autobiography:

> It's the same thing as if one of my children was kidnapped and there was a demand for ransom. Sure, I don't believe in ransom, because it leads to more kidnapping. But if I find out there's somebody who has access to the kidnapper and can get my child back without doing anything for the kidnapper, I'd sure do that.[77]

The United States also feared that when the elderly Khomeini died, the Soviets might take advantage of the confusion over who would lead Iran next in order to increase their influence in the region. To avoid this possibility, America sought a way to develop relations with moderate members of the government, and offering to sell them weapons was one way to gain influence.

When National Security Advisor Robert McFarlane mentioned in August 1985 that moderate members of the Iranian government would gain the release of the seven American hostages in return for U.S. weapons, Reagan was very interested. He wanted to get the captives home at any cost, even if it meant selling arms to terrorists.

Both Secretary of State George Shultz and Secretary of Defense Caspar Weinberger told the president that the arms sales were a bad idea. Shultz said, ominously, that "the whole story will come out someday and we will pay the price."[78] But Reagan was reluctant to pass up any opportunity to gain the release of hostages. He approved the arms sales to Iran over the objections of his most experienced advisors.

The first delivery of missiles was made in August of 1985—and the Iranians refused to release any of the hostages. Iran then demanded four hundred more missiles before they would free Americans. When the missiles were delivered as promised in September, Iran released just one hostage in return.

ARMS-FOR-HOSTAGES

Ronald Reagan recalls the fierce opposition from members of his staff to selling arms to Iran in exchange for the release of American hostages. He also explains in his autobiography his decision to proceed with the arms-for-hostages trade.

". . . while Cap [Caspar Weinberger] and George [Shultz] disagreed on many topics, they were united on one thing: Almost from the day Bud McFarlane brought us the proposal for arms sales to Iran, they were against it. They warned me against participating in any arrangement that might be interpreted as linking the shipment of arms with efforts to free the hostages. At that meeting on Pearl Harbor Day, 1985, when we considered continuing and possibly even expanding the covert operation begun the previous summer, they made their opposition clear to me forcefully. They didn't argue that the plan involved a swap of arms for hostages, but they contended that if information ever leaked out (and George insisted that it would), it would be made to *look* as if we were.

My response to them was that we were *not* trading arms for hostages, nor were we negotiating with terrorists . . .

'Look,' I said, 'we all agree we can't pay ransom to the Hizballah to get the hostages. But we are not dealing with the Hizballah, we are not doing a thing for them. We are trying to help some people who are looking forward to becoming the next government of Iran, and they are getting the weapons in return for saying that they are going to try to use their influence to free our hostages. It's the same thing as if one of my children was kidnapped and there was a demand for ransom; sure, I don't believe in ransom because it leads to more kidnapping. But if I find out there's somebody who has access to the kidnapper and can get my child back without doing anything for the kidnapper, I'd sure do that."

The shipments continued despite Iran's failure to hold up its end of the bargain. In November, more missiles were delivered to Iran, and again, no Americans were freed. The scene was repeated several months later, after a delivery of one thousand missiles. As McFarlane prepared to accompany Reagan to the November 1985 Geneva nuclear arms negotiations with Gorbachev, he decided to turn the arms-for-hostages operation over to Oliver North, the same man who had helped him secretly support the contras.

"A NEAT IDEA"

Oliver North had made his reputation as a soldier in the Vietnam War, where he was wounded twice and awarded several medals for heroism in combat. His patriotism was indisputable, but many of Reagan's advisors had doubts about his judgment. Michael Deaver, for one, placed North on his list of people who should be kept out of Reagan's office. Later, Deaver would try to explain why he tried to prevent North from seeing the president:

A U.S. soldier handles a portable missile launcher. In 1985, Reagan agreed to sell arms to Iran in return for the release of U.S. hostages.

I guess I'm cynical, or suspicious, but he [North] was exactly the kind of guy I wouldn't want around. He was kind of bright-eyed and bushy-tailed, and "Yes, sir," and "No, sir," and wore the flag on his heart. Reagan was very impressed with him because he was exactly that kind of all-American kid. In many ways Reagan could see everything; in other ways he could be a fool.[79]

After McFarlane resigned in December 1985, citing stress and illness, John Poindexter took over as national security advisor. North in turn took on even more responsibility for the arms sales to Iran. When the first sale under his supervision turned a profit of several hundred thousand dollars, North had what he later described as "a neat idea."[80] With the help of an ex–Air Force general named Richard Secord, he decided to use the money to buy weapons for the contras in Nicaragua.

A sale of missiles to Iran in early 1986 netted more than $6 million in profit, which North again directed toward the cause of the contras. Later, North went so far as to overcharge the Iranians for the weapons so that he had more money left over for the contras. The arms shipments did not have the intended effect of gaining the freedom of American hostages, but they offered an opportunity to buy more weapons and supplies for the Nicaraguan rebels without having to ask for congressional approval.

Even while members of his administration were selling arms to Iran, Reagan repeated his promise that he would never give in to the demands of international terrorists. In April of 1986, he ordered an air attack on Libya, which he held responsible for the bombing of a West German disco club that killed an American soldier. The American public showed strong support for the military response to terrorists.

The Scandal Is Exposed

In October of 1986, a cargo plane full of weapons and supplies bound for the contras was shot down by the Sandanistas. The surviving crew member, a former CIA employee named Eugene Hasenfus, told his captors that the downed flight was part of a secret American operation. The crewman's story appeared in the international press, and reporters made the link between North and Hasenfus. The Iran-contra connection was exposed.

CIA director William Casey, John Poindexter, Oliver North, and President Reagan denied all allegations initially. They believed that the story would quickly blow over. In mid-November, Reagan publicly downplayed the Iran-contra link, saying firmly, "We did not—repeat did not—trade weapons or anything else for hostages nor will we."[81]

Meanwhile, many of Reagan's advisors urged him to reveal publicly what he knew about the Iran-contra affair. They remembered how, during the Watergate scandal of the early 1970s, President Nixon had been damaged the most not by his original misconduct but by his later attempts to cover it up.

Attorney General Ed Meese began an internal investigation into the matter, but he

BARRY GOLDWATER SPEAKS OUT

In an April 9, 1984 letter to Central Intelligence Agency director William Casey, reprinted in Haynes Johnson's Sleepwalking Through History, *Arizona senator Barry Goldwater expresses his anger at Reagan's continued illegal support for the Nicaraguan contras.*

"Dear Bill:

All this past weekend, I've been trying to figure out how I can most easily tell you my feelings about the discovery of the President having approved mining some of the harbors of Central America.

It gets down to one, little, simple phrase: I am pissed off!

. . .

Bill, this is no way to run a railroad, and I find myself in a hell of a quandary. I am forced to apologize to the Members of the Intelligence Committee because I did not know the facts on this. . . .

The President has asked us to back his foreign policy. Bill, how can we back his foreign policy when we don't know what the hell he is doing? Lebanon, yes, we all knew that he sent troops over there. But mine the harbors in Nicaragua? This is an act violating international law. It is an act of war. For the life of me, I don't see how we are going to explain it. . . .

I don't like this. I don't like it one bit from the President or from you. I don't think we need a lot of lengthy explanations. The deed has been done and, in the future, if anything like this happens, I'm going to raise one hell of a lot of fuss about it in public."

failed to move quickly enough to gather key documents. Aware that Meese's probe was under way, North had enough time to undertake what he called a "shredding party."[82] North later admitted in congressional testimony that he spent two days destroying documents related to the arms sales in his office's paper-shredding machine, with the help of his secretary Fawn Hall and his deputy Robert Earl.

Meese's inquiry did uncover a memo from North to Poindexter about the use of arms sales profits to aid the contras. The finding was enough to finally convince Reagan that the scandal could no longer be covered up.

At a November 25, 1986, press conference, Reagan admitted, without discussing his own involvement, that there was some evidence of an arms-for-hostages deal. He said that he was "deeply troubled that the implementation of a policy aimed at resolving a truly tragic situation in the Middle East had resulted in such controversy."[83] Reagan accepted Poindexter's resignation on the same day. He also fired North, but not before thanking him for his service. "Ollie, you're a national hero," the president said.[84]

However, Reagan's admission that an arms-for-hostages exchange took place was not enough to salvage his sagging reputation. Ninety percent of people surveyed in a *Newsweek* poll said they believed Reagan was still lying about the Iran-contra affair. A *New York Times*/CBS poll taken on December 2 showed that his public approval rating had plummeted from 67 percent to 46 percent, the biggest one-month drop for a president since such polling began a half century before.[85]

THE TOWER COMMISSION

His credibility questioned by the public, Reagan responded by establishing the Tower Commission in December of 1986. The three members of the commission—former senator John Tower, former secretary of state Edmund Muskie, and former national security advisor Brent Scowcroft—were instructed to delve deeper into the arms sales to Iran.

The Tower Commission's investigation immediately ran into obstacles. William Casey, who had been heavily involved in the covert activities, was hospitalized with a brain tumor that would soon prove fatal. Former national security advisor Robert McFarlane, another key figure, attempted suicide in the midst of his testimony. Poindexter and North refused to testify before the commission.

Reagan's own appearances before the commission did little to clarify the issue. In his January 26, 1987, testimony, he stated that he had approved arms sales to Iran in August of 1985, which was consistent with McFarlane's testimony. But he changed his testimony when he met with the Tower Commission three weeks later, telling them that he had no advance knowledge of the arms sales. On February 20, he changed his testimony yet again. "I have no personal notes or records to help my recollection on this matter," he told the commission. "My answer therefore and the simple truth is, 'I don't remember, period.'"[86]

The Tower Commission believed the president and in its written report of February 26 did not directly blame him for the Iran-contra scandal. The president, said John Tower in a statement issued with the report, "clearly didn't understand the nature of this operation, who was involved, and what was happening."[87] The report did hurt Reagan's public image, however, by portraying him as a detached leader who had little awareness or understanding of his staff's activities.

Two weeks after the Tower report came out, Reagan finally admitted to the public that he traded arms for hostages. "A few months ago I told the American people I did not trade arms for hostages," he said in a March 4 speech. "My heart and my best intentions still tell me that's true, but the facts and evidence tell me it is not."[88]

Reagan, seen here with former senator John Tower, established the Tower Commission for the purpose of investigating the Iran-contra scandal.

Only once would he offer anything resembling an apology for the Iran-contra affair. In a March 1987 speech, Reagan said, "What had begun as a strategic opening to Iran deteriorated, in its implementation, into trading arms for hostages. It was a mistake."[89]

A ten-month investigation by the House and Senate did not produce conclusive evidence that Reagan was aware of the full extent of the Iran-contra operation, including the diversion of profits from the arms sales to the contras. But the congressional report placed final responsibility for the scandal on the president. "If the President did not know what his National Security Advisors were doing, he should have," the report stated.[90]

Lawrence Walsh, an independent counsel appointed to conduct a third investigation into the Iran-contra affair, ultimately charged fourteen people with criminal violations. North was found guilty of three felony counts of obstructing Congress, destroying documents, and accepting an illegal gratuity. Poindexter was convicted on five felony counts of conspiracy, lying to Congress, and obstruction of the congressional investigation. The Supreme Court later overturned Poindexter's and North's convictions on technical grounds.

During their trials, both North and Poindexter gave damaging testimony about the president's level of involvement in the scandal. North's statements were particularly harmful: "I would not have done any of this if I had thought for a minute that the president of the United States had not approved it. . . . I believed then, and I believe today, that the president knew exactly what was going on."[91]

In 1987, Poindexter told congressional investigators that the president had no knowledge of the illegal acts. But he changed his testimony during his 1990 trial, stating that the president knew all of the details of the arms sales to Iran and the diversion of funds to the contras. Under oath, Poindexter said that he had given Reagan daily updates on the status of the covert operations.

The belief that Reagan had been involved in at least some aspect of the Iran-contra affair was shared by some of his most loyal supporters. Secretary of State George Shultz believed that the president knew at the very least about the sale of arms to Iran. "There isn't any doubt that the president signed on as far as the arms sales were concerned," Shultz later said.[92] The president himself created strong evidence supporting Shultz' belief. A January 17, 1986, notation in Reagan's diary reads: "I agreed to sell TOWs [antitank missiles] to Iran."[93]

DAMAGE CONTROL

With the Iran-contra affair now out in the open, Reagan attempted to regain the public's trust. He forced out his chief of staff Donald Regan, who was also under fire from Nancy Reagan for his failure to protect the president from the scandal. Regan's replacement was Howard Baker,

a level-headed former senator from Tennessee. Reagan also hired highly respected replacements for Poindexter and for other staff members tarnished by the Iran-contra scandal.

The biggest boost for Reagan's reputation came when he and Gorbachev signed the INF nuclear weapons treaty in December 1987. The public showed great enthusiasm for Reagan's efforts to end the nuclear arms race, and opinion polls showed that his popularity was once again on the rise. By the time he returned from his trip to Moscow in 1988, his approval rating reached 70 percent, as high as it had ever been.

THE END OF THE REVOLUTION

Unfortunately for Reagan and other conservatives, the Iran-contra affair made it difficult for him to accomplish anything in the domestic policy arena. Reagan had enjoyed such widespread popularity in his first term that even the Democrat-controlled House of Representatives felt that it was politically necessary to support his conservative proposals, including cuts in social welfare programs and increased military spending.

But as Reagan's popularity plummeted throughout most of 1987, the Democrats were able to pursue their own agenda more aggressively. In addition, the 1986 elections had left them with majority control of both the House and Senate. Throughout 1987 and into 1988, the Democrats passed dozens of laws, many of which reversed conservative changes Reagan had made during his first term. They enacted bills supporting fair housing, the homeless, and public school education. They expanded civil rights protections, environmental laws, and the food stamp program.

Every time Reagan used his veto power to defeat the liberal proposals, the Democrats were able to gather the votes needed to override his veto. And in October 1987, Congress rejected Robert Bork as Reagan's nominee to the Supreme Court—the first time a presidential nomination to the Supreme Court had been rejected since the Nixon administration. The president, who had seemed unstoppable while pushing conservative policy initiatives through Congress in his first term, had lost much of his political power.

Chapter

7 Reagan's Legacy

On January 20, 1989, Ronald Reagan took a last look around the Oval Office and received a final briefing from National Security Advisor Colin Powell.

Vice President George Bush became president in 1989.

"The world is quiet today, Mr. President," said Powell.[94] With his wife at his side, Reagan boarded a helicopter to begin the long journey home to California. Seventy-eight years old, and prevented by the Constitution from seeking a third term in office, he was returning to private life. In elections the previous November, American voters had selected his vice president, George Bush, to take his place.

Reagan left behind a nation that was stronger in many ways than it had been eight years before. He also left behind opposing armies of admirers and critics and a fierce debate over the lasting legacies of the Reagan years.

THE END OF THE COLD WAR AND THE COLLAPSE OF COMMUNISM

At the beginning of his presidency, few would have guessed that Reagan would sign the first treaty ever to reduce American and Soviet nuclear weapon arsenals. But despite his harsh criticisms of the Soviet Union and aggressive moves to build up America's armed forces, Reagan believed firmly that, "A nuclear war can never be won and must never be fought."[95] As he wrote in his autobiography:

> My dream, then, became a world free of nuclear weapons.
>
> Some of my advisors, including a number at the Pentagon, did not share this dream. They couldn't conceive of it. They said that a nuclear-free world was unattainable and it would be dangerous for us even if it were possible; some even claimed nuclear war was "inevitable" and we had to prepare for this reality. . . . But for the eight years I was president I never let my dream of a nuclear-free world fade from my mind.[96]

The 1987 signing of the INF nuclear arms reduction agreement with Gorbachev was an important step toward this dream. It signaled the end of the Cold War, and other even bigger changes to come.

As early as 1982, Reagan had confidently predicted that the communist system of government was doomed to failure, and the events of the late 1980s seemed to prove him right. In June of 1987, he gave a speech in front of the Brandenburg Gate of the Berlin Wall—the wall built in 1949 to divide communist East Berlin from democratic West Berlin, and the most important symbol of the Cold War divide: "*General Secretary Gorbachev, if you seek peace, if you seek prosperity for the Soviet Union and Eastern Europe, if you seek liberalization: Come here to this gate! Mr. Gorbachev, open this gate! Mr. Gorbachev, tear down this wall!*"[97]

A little over two years later, the Berlin Wall was torn down, and the two halves of Germany were reunited. With its economy in shambles, the Soviet Union could no longer afford to maintain its iron grip on East Germany and other communist countries. The communist governments of Eastern Europe fell from power one after another during the winter of 1989–1990. Poland's Solidarity Party came to power after ten years of struggle against communist rule. In Czechoslovakia, a writer and human rights advocate named Václav Havel was elected president. The communist rulers of Hungary, Bulgaria, Lithuania, Romania, and Yugoslavia either resigned or were replaced.

In June 1987 Reagan gave a speech in front of the Brandenburg Gate in Berlin encouraging Gorbachev to end the Cold War separation of Germany.

STRONG WORDS AT THE BERLIN WALL

On June 12, 1987, Reagan made a powerful speech in front of the Brandenburg Gate of the Berlin Wall, the most visible symbol of the Cold War. He demanded that Gorbachev remove the wall as a symbol of his commitment to world peace. The speech appears in Reagan's autobiography.

". . . After these four decades, then, there stands before the entire world one great and inescapable conclusion: Freedom leads to prosperity. Freedom replaces the ancient hatreds among the nations with comity and peace. Freedom is the victor. And now the Soviets themselves may, in a limited way, be coming to understand the importance of freedom. We hear much now from Moscow about a new policy of reform and openness. Some political prisoners have been released. Certain foreign news broadcasts are no longer being jammed. Some economic enterprises have been permitted to operate with greater freedom from state control.

Are these the beginnings of profound changes in the Soviet state? Or are they token gestures, intended to raise false hopes in the West, or to strengthen the Soviet System without changing it? We welcome change and openness; for we believe that freedom and security go together, that the advance of human liberty can only strengthen the cause of world peace. There is one sign the Soviets can make that would be unmistakable, that would advance dramatically the cause of freedom and peace. . . .

General Secretary Gorbachev, if you seek peace, if you seek prosperity for the Soviet Union and Eastern Europe, if you seek liberalization: Come here to this gate! Mr. Gorbachev, open this gate! Mr. Gorbachev, tear down this wall!"

Next to assert their independence were the collection of republics that made up the Soviet Union itself; Estonia, Georgia, and the Ukraine were the first to break away. Meanwhile, Gorbachev chipped away at the Communist Party rule with his reforms—but not quickly enough to save his job. In August of 1991, an attempted coup severely weakened Gorbachev's grip on power, leading to the breakup of the USSR in January 1992.

Reagan's admirers credit his anticommunist policies with helping to bring about the collapse of the Soviet Union. Critics argue that the Soviet economy was in such poor shape that the collapse was unavoidable.

Regardless of who deserves the credit, the fall of the Soviet Union marked the end of an era. For fifty years, the Soviets posed a moral, military, and ideological threat to America. Containing this threat was the most important goal for every president from Truman to Reagan. And now the threat was gone, taking with it the troubling chance of nuclear war between the world's two superpowers. As the 1990s began, the world was a safer place.

THE LEGACY OF REAGANOMICS

Reagan also left a lasting mark on America's domestic policies and programs. In 1981, the new president promised to fix the ailing economy with Reaganomics, a combination of lower taxes and sharp reductions in the size and power of the federal government. Eight years later, Reagan could claim many economic victories. Inflation and interest rates dropped during his administration, and 18 million new jobs were created. According to a poll taken when he left office, 62 percent of those surveyed approved of his handling of the economy. By these standards, the economy was thriving, enjoying the longest peacetime expansion in American history.

Martin Anderson, an advisor in both the Nixon and Reagan administrations, wrote that Reaganomics marked a critical change in American political thinking:

> What Reagan and his comrades have done is to shape America's political agenda well into the 21st century. . . . We are now following a new path . . .

one marked by a heightened appreciation of the need for a strong national defense, the desirability of low tax rates and minimal government regulation, and a greater prosperity and sense of national confidence.[98]

Reagan's ideas about the economy continue to guide American politics. American politicians must be careful to avoid the higher taxes and increased government regulations that Reagan spoke out against. And in doing so, they are sometimes unable to make changes they believe would be good for the nation. Author William Pemberton describes the problems President Bill Clinton experienced in 1993 as he tried to reform the nation's troubled health care system:

> The first Reagan legacy, hatred of taxes, prevented Clinton from proposing the tax increase necessary to fund the kind of program he believed the nation needed. He then tried to substitute government regulation of the health care system for adequate financing and that ran into the second Reagan legacy: distrust of government.[99]

SHRINKING GOVERNMENT?

While the ideas behind Reaganomics remain a political force in America today, Reagan himself was not always able to put them into practice. For example, Reagan failed in his attempts to shrink the size of the federal government, one of the basic goals of his economic program. The

REAGAN ON REAGANOMICS

In his autobiography, Reagan defends himself against the charge that his economic program was responsible for a massive budget deficit.

"With the tax cuts of 1981 and the Tax Reform Act of 1986, I'd accomplished a lot of what I'd come to Washington to do.

But on the other side of the ledger, cutting federal spending and balancing the budget, I was less successful than I wanted to be. This was one of my biggest disappointments as president. I just didn't deliver as much to the people as I'd promised.

I never thought we could cut costs so fast that we'd balance the budget overnight. I knew it would take time. There were too many programs that people based their lives and businesses on; you couldn't pull the rug out from under all of them at once. But I wanted to cut more of the waste that had accumulated in government like flab around the waist of a middle-aged man.

I didn't come to Washington with stars in my eyes, thinking it would be easy. I'd been through the same kind of battle at the state level and knew how difficult it could be. I came to Washington thinking that it was going to be tough, but that it could be done.

Over time, we rendered a lot of fat out of the government; we reduced the size of the bureaucracy and cut the rate at which the government was growing and spending money, and I'm very proud of that. But the vested interests that hold sway over Congress prevented us from cutting spending nearly as much as I had hoped to, or as the country required."

number of government employees increased at a faster rate under him than under the Carter administration. The federal government spent $1.9 trillion more during the Reagan years than it would have if spending had remained at 1980 levels. At the same time, the national debt tripled during his administration, another indication of Reagan's inability to control the government's size and spending habits.

Deregulation, Reagan's campaign to relax federal control of corporations, also

Reagan gives a press conference regarding the presence of Soviet fighter planes in Cuba. The Soviet Union would soon fall, and the world would be a safer place.

met with mixed results. While it may have helped wake the economy from its slumber, it also left behind some major problems, including the savings-and-loan (S&L) crisis.

S&Ls were originally established to make federally insured loans to companies and individuals. In 1982, the Reagan administration relaxed the rules on S&Ls, allowing them to make risky investments with government-insured money. According to *U.S. News and World Report*, deregulation turned S&Ls into:

> a huge casino where only taxpayers could lose. . . . Many S&L kingpins lived like royalty, buying opulent homes, yachts and political influence. Cronies and insiders obtained huge loans with little collateral. . . . And

many of those who weren't deliberately pillaging their S&Ls were simply lousy business operators, investing in everything from bull-sperm banks to shopping centers in the desert.[100]

When the risky investments and loans soured, the federal government had to clean up the mess. A 1996 assessment by the General Accounting Office found that the S&L bailout had already cost the government more than $480 billion, and could cost hundreds of billions more, making it by far the most costly government-caused scandal in history.

REAGANOMICS AND THE POOR

The rich got richer under Reaganomics, thanks in large part to the tax cuts he pushed through Congress. The number of people reporting income over $1 million went from forty-four hundred in 1980 to thirty-five thousand in 1987, and the wealthiest one-fifth of Americans saw their income leap upward by 15 percent over the same period.

Although Reaganomics worked for the wealthy, it also left many people behind. The poverty rate reached 14 percent of the population in 1989, some 33 million people. The poorest 20 percent of Americans saw their income drop by 7 percent during the Reagan administration. The gap between the rich and the poor grew wider than it had been in forty years.

At the same time, cuts in government programs made it harder for the poor to get help. In the year after Reagan made his first welfare reforms, over 1 million poor people became ineligible for Medicaid and Aid to Families with Dependent Children, two critical assistance programs. The Housing and Urban Development Department (HUD), which was created to provide the poor with affordable housing, saw its budget chopped from $33 billion to $14 billion from 1981 to 1987. To make matters worse, a 1990 investigation found that the agency had misused several billion dollars during the Reagan administration. HUD officials used federal money intended for the construction of low-income housing to build luxury apartments, pools, and golf courses.

Growing poverty is often matched by increases in crime and drug abuse, and the 1980s were no exception. Murders in the United States topped twenty thousand a year, the highest in the world. Drugs became a staggering problem, with the use of cocaine and crack cocaine reaching epidemic proportions. The administration responded with more funding for law enforcement, which in turn led to record numbers of drug busts and convictions—the number of people in prison doubled during the 1980s.

THE SPREAD OF AIDS

AIDS, a disease affecting the immune system, also cut a deadly path across America during the Reagan years. The number of AIDS-related deaths in the United States, thirty-seven hundred at the beginning of Reagan's first term, rocketed up to more than forty-six thousand four years later. By the time he left office in 1989, fifty-five thousand Americans had died from complications of the disease. Blacks, gays, poor people, and intravenous drug users were hardest hit.

Even though the scope of the problem was recognized early on, the Reagan administration was slow to support AIDS research or public education programs. C. Everett Koop, Reagan's surgeon general, recalled that he was ordered to stay away from the issue.

> I was told I had so much on my plate that AIDS would not be expected to be under my purview, and that I was to keep out of that, and that other people would handle it. . . . It was a discouraging time. Occasionally when I went for meetings in the White House where AIDS was discussed at a lower level—or at several cabinet meetings where it was discussed—the

AIDS and the Reagan Administration

C. Everett Koop was the Surgeon General of the United States under Reagan. He was deeply disturbed by the Reagan administration's slow reaction to the rapid spread of the deadly AIDS virus through the U.S. population. He is quoted in Deborah H. Strober and Gerald S. Strober's Reagan: The Man and His Presidency.

"I was told I had so much on my plate that AIDS would not be expected to be under my purview, and that I was to keep out of that, and that other people would handle it.
. . .

I suspect that he [Reagan] was told, 'AIDS is something you don't have to worry about, Mr. President, because, after all, it affects homosexuals, it affects drug abusers, it affects sexually promiscuous people, Mr. President. And these are not your people.'

I wasn't there to hear that, but that is what I suspect, because I know that is what a lot of the people around him felt. And he was also surrounded by a lot of people who thought that sex education was the worst thing that could happen to America. And some of them actually told me, to my face, that I was leading the children of America down the garden path to immorality.

It was a discouraging time. Occasionally when I went for meetings in the White House where AIDS was discussed at a lower level—or at several cabinet meetings where it was discussed—the reaction of the people around the table was not modern, was not scientific, was not compassionate, and was not realistic. . . .

I think that they truly believed that if you ignored it, it could go away. I don't think that the people around Reagan ever understood the seriousness of the epidemic, and I don't know whether they have yet caught on as to how many people have died in this country, how many are infected, and what the world situation is—which is an absolute, ghastly tragedy."

reaction of the people around the table was not modern, was not scientific, was not compassionate, and was not realistic.[101]

Some members of Reagan's staff believed that AIDS was a punishment for what were in their opinion immoral behaviors such as drug use and homosexuality.

As Chief of Staff Donald Regan said: "The Reagan administration realized that there was an AIDS crisis, but that it was being caused by immoral practices. And how far do we want to go to make the world safe for immoral practices?"[103]

Reagan finally became concerned in 1985 when his friend and fellow actor Rock Hudson died from complications of the disease. But even after Hudson's death, Reagan rarely spoke about the disease in public. While Margaret Thatcher launched a public information campaign about AIDS in Britain, Reagan's silence limited public awareness and hindered efforts to control the spread of the deadly disease.

THE CONSERVATIVE LEGACY

Members of the New Right, the ultraconservative voters who helped put Reagan into office in 1980 and 1984, hoped that the president would do more than just fix the economy. They wanted Reagan to follow through on his conservative campaign promises, including the introduction of prayer to public schools and a constitutional ban on abortion.

Once in office, Reagan did not spend much time and effort trying to ban abortion or secure a constitutional amendment to allow prayer in schools. He chose to save his political influence to support eco-

In order to keep liberals at bay, Reagan appointed three conservatives to the Supreme Court. One of them was Sandra Day O'Connor (seen here with Reagan), the first female member of the Supreme Court.

nomic and foreign policy goals and steered clear of these controversial issues. As a result, his track record as president was less conservative than the New Right had hoped.

On most issues, however, Reagan's policies were reliably conservative. Conservative supporters were generally pleased by Reagan's campaign to cut taxes and welfare programs and increase military spending. They were also satisfied with his efforts to ensure that the nation's legal system moved in a more conservative direction. Reagan had the opportunity to appoint more federal judges than any president in history, and his appointments shared his conservative views against abortion and were in favor of the death penalty and stiff sentences for criminals.

Reagan's three appointments to the nine-member Supreme Court, the highest legal authority in the United States, were solid conservatives. Reagan believed that the Supreme Court had bowed to liberals in the 1960s and 1970s by supporting legal abortion and more rights for criminals and minorities. To reverse this trend, in 1981 Reagan nominated Sandra Day O'Connor, a conservative Arizona appeals court judge and former state senator, as the first female member of the Supreme Court. When Chief Justice Warren Burger resigned in 1986, Reagan promoted the court's most conservative member, William Rehnquist, to chief justice. He named another conservative, Antonin Scalia, to fill the vacancy. Finally, Reagan appointed California conservative Anthony Kennedy when Lewis Powell resigned in 1987.

With these additions, the Supreme Court became more conservative in the 1980s. Homosexuals were turned back in their attempts to gain legal protections, for example, and rulings that limited police authority were overturned. However, Reagan's appointments have not resulted in a conservative shift on other key issues. The Supreme Court continues to uphold the right to an abortion, defend free speech, and maintain the division between church and state.

The Symbolic Presidency

The successes and failures of the Reagan administration can be debated endlessly, but the strength of Reagan's appeal to many Americans is indisputable. He was the first president in thirty years to complete two terms in the White House, and he departed more popular than any exiting president since Franklin Roosevelt.

He left office with his popularity intact despite the drawn-out scandal of the Iran-contra affair, which had left the public with images of a confused and detached president. He retained his popularity despite a frequent gap between his words and his actions, and a reputation for public misstatements so large that entire books were published on the subject. Reagan's success in cutting taxes, righting the economy and making peace with the Soviet Union—issues that were tremendously important to the American people—explains part of his popularity. Reagan's importance as a symbol may explain the rest.

Reagan's life encompasses many of the most important events in America during the twentieth century. His own experiences touched on the Great Depression, Hollywood, the American West, and World War II. He was a symbol of values that had been an important part of America for generations—patriotism, God, strong morals, and the rags-to-riches promise of America. In his book *Reagan's America*, Gary Wills calls him, "a perfect blend of an authentic America he grew up in and that of America's own fables about its past."[102] Reagan was also aware of why he was so appealing to the American people:

> I've always thought of myself as a citizen politician, speaking up for the ideas and values and common sense of everyday Americans. That's what I've always tried to do, and maybe that's what it is they [the people] like.[103]

Americans seemed willing to forgive Reagan's missteps and misstatements, so powerful was their affection for what he symbolized. And in doing so, they could believe in his vision of a brighter future for America. Even in the most difficult times of his presidency, Reagan remained calm, optimistic, and cheerful. Conservative commentator George Will believed that the cheerfulness and optimism masked serious problems facing the country; he called the president's sunny disposition "a narcotic that numbed the nation's senses to the hazards over the horizon."[104]

But many Americans were cheered and reassured by Reagan's confident leadership. In his last presidential address, on January 11, 1989, he left the public with a final optimistic vision of America, comparing the nation to a shining city on a hill:

> a tall proud city built on rocks stronger than oceans, wind-swept, God-blessed, and teeming with people of all kinds living in harmony and peace, a city with free ports that hummed with commerce and creativity, and if there had to be city walls, the walls had doors and the doors were open to anyone with the will and the heart to get there. That's how I saw it, and see it still.[105]

Notes

Introduction: Reagan Takes the Stage

1. Quoted in Lou Cannon, *President Reagan: The Role of a Lifetime*. New York: Simon and Schuster, 1991, p. 830.

2. Quoted in Bob Schieffer and Gary Paul Gates, *The Acting President*. New York: Dutton, 1989, p. 14.

3. D. Erik Felton, ed., *A Shining City: The Legacy of Ronald Reagan*. New York: Simon and Schuster, 1998, p. 20.

Chapter One: The Road to the White House

4. Quoted in Schieffer and Gates, *The Acting President*, p. 14.

5. Quoted in William E. Pemberton, *Exit with Honor: The Life and Presidency of Ronald Reagan*. Armonk, NY: M. E. Sharpe, 1997, p. 7.

6. Ronald Reagan, *An American Life: The Autobiography of Ronald Reagan*. New York: Simon and Schuster, 1990, p. 29.

7. Reagan, *An American Life*, p. 231.

8. Reagan, *An American Life*, p. 110.

9. Ronald Reagan, *Speaking My Mind*. New York: Simon and Schuster, 1989, p. 36.

10. Quoted in Schieffer and Gates, *The Acting President*, p. 14.

11. Reagan, *Speaking My Mind*, p. 412.

12. Reagan, *An American Life*, p. 219.

13. Quoted in Robert Dallek, *Ronald Reagan, The Politics of Symbolism*. Cambridge, MA: Harvard University Press, 1984, p. 57.

14. Quoted in L. B. Taylor Jr., *The New Right*. New York: Franklin Watts, 1981, p. 28.

15. Quoted in Taylor, *The New Right*, p. 29.

16. Quoted in Taylor, *The New Right*, p. 13.

17. Reagan, *Speaking My Mind*, p. 62.

Chapter Two: Reaganomics in Action

18. Quoted in Cannon, *President Reagan: The Role of a Lifetime*, p. 77.

19. Reagan, *Speaking My Mind*, p. 82.

20. Quoted in Pemberton, *Exit with Honor*, p. 208.

21. Quoted in Fred I. Greenstein, ed., *The Reagan Presidency: An Early Assessment*. Baltimore: John Hopkins University Press, 1983, p. 59.

22. Quoted in Dallek, *Ronald Reagan, The Politics of Symbolism*, p. 69.

23. Quoted in Schieffer and Gates, *The Acting President*, p. 102.

24. Quoted in Dallek, *Ronald Reagan, The Politics of Symbolism*, p. 71.

25. Quoted in Michael Schaller, *Reckoning with Reagan: America and Its President in the 1980s*. New York: Oxford University Press, 1992, p. 100.

26. Quoted in Dallek, *Ronald Reagan, The Politics of Symbolism*, p. 100.

27. Quoted in Dallek, *Ronald Reagan, The Politics of Symbolism*, p. 102.

28. Quoted in Dallek, *Ronald Reagan, The Politics of Symbolism*, p. 100.

29. Quoted in Dallek, *Ronald Reagan, The Politics of Symbolism*, p. 113.

30. Quoted in Schaller, *Reckoning With Reagan*, p. 43.

Chapter Three: The Cold Warrior

31. Quoted in Laurence I. Barrett, *Gambling with History: Reagan in the White House*. New York: Penguin Books, 1984, p. 297.

32. Quoted in Cannon, *President Reagan*, p. 320.

33. Quoted in Greenstein, *The Reagan Presidency*, p. 141.

34. Quoted in Dallek, *Ronald Reagan, The Politics of Symbolism*, p. 153.

35. Quoted in Barrett, *Gambling with History*, p. 320.

36. Quoted in Dallek, *Ronald Reagan, The Politics of Symbolism*, p. 160.

37. Quoted in Schaller, *Reckoning with Reagan*, p. 131.

38. Quoted in Barrett, *Gambling with History*, p. 324.

39. Quoted in Cannon, *President Reagan*, p. 316.

40. Quoted in Dallek, *Ronald Reagan, The Politics of Symbolism*, p. 159.

41. Quoted in Schaller, *Reckoning with Reagan*, p. 133.

Chapter Four: Trouble Abroad

42. Quoted in Dallek, *Ronald Reagan, The Politics of Symbolism*, p. 141.

43. Reagan, *An American Life*, p. 292.

44. Reagan, *An American Life*, p. 291.

45. Quoted in Dallek, *Ronald Reagan, The Politics of Symbolism*, p. 171.

46. Reagan, *Speaking My Mind*, p. 190.

47. Quoted in Cannon, *President Reagan*, p. 445.

48. Quoted in Cannon, *President Reagan*, p. 445.

49. Quoted in Cannon, *President Reagan*, p. 449.

50. Quoted in Cannon, *President Reagan*, p. 471.

51. Quoted in Cannon, *President Reagan*, p. 484.

Chapter Five: Four More Years

52. Quoted in Cannon, *President Reagan*, p. 217.

53. Quoted in Cannon, *President Reagan*, p. 515.

54. Quoted in Cannon, *President Reagan*, p. 512–13.

55. Quoted in Deborah H. Strober and Gerald S. Strober, *Reagan: The Man and His Presidency*. Boston: Houghton Mifflin Company, 1998, p. 303.

56. Quoted in William A. Degregorio, *The Complete Book of U.S. Presidents*. New York: Random House, 1997, p. 646.

57. Quoted in David W. Houck and Amos Kiewe, *A Shining City on a Hill: Ronald Reagan's Economic Rhetoric, 1951–1989*. New York: Praeger, 1991, p. 166.

58. Quoted in Schaller, *Reckoning with Reagan*, p. 147.

59. Quoted in Schieffer and Gates, *The Acting President*, p. 189.

60. Quoted in Schieffer and Gates, *The Acting President*, p. 95.

61. Quoted in Schieffer and Gates, *The Acting President*, p. 90.

62. Quoted in Jane Mayer and Doyle McManus, *Landslide: The Unmaking of the President 1984–1988*. Boston: Houghton Mifflin Company, 1988, p. 36.

63. Quoted in Mayer and McManus, *Landslide*, p. 19.

64. Quoted in Michael Mendelbaum and Strobe Talbott, *Reagan and Gorbachev: The Chances for a Breakthrough in U.S.-Soviet Relations*. New York: Vintage Books, 1987, p. 44.

65. Quoted in Mendelbaum and Talbott, *Reagan and Gorbachev*, p. 43.

66. Reagan, *An American Life*, p. 615.

67. Quoted in Cannon, *President Reagan*, p. 770.

68. Quoted in Cannon, *President Reagan*, p. 782.

69. Quoted in Schieffer and Gates, *The Acting President*, p. 334.

Chapter Six: The Iran-Contra Affair

70. Quoted in Cannon, *President Reagan*, p. 611.

71. Quoted in Haynes Johnson, *Sleepwalking Through History: America in the Reagan Years*. New York: W. W. Norton and Company, 1991, p. 276.

72. Quoted in Cannon, *President Reagan*, p. 366.

73. Quoted in Schaller, *Reckoning with Reagan*, p. 152.

74. Quoted in Johnson, *Sleepwalking Through History*, p. 280.

75. Quoted in Pemberton, *Exit with Honor*, p. 276.

76. Quoted in Pemberton, *Exit with Honor*, p. 177.

77. Quoted in Pemberton, *Exit with Honor*, p. 177.

78. Quoted in Pemberton, *Exit with Honor*, p. 183.

79. Quoted in Strober and Strober, *Reagan*, p. 515.

80. Quoted in Renée Schwartzberg, *Ronald Reagan*. New York: Chelsea House Publishers, 1991, p. 113.

81. Quoted in Schaller, *Reckoning with Reagan*, p. 164.

82. Quoted in Schieffer and Gates, *The Acting President*, p. 290.

83. Quoted in Cannon, *President Reagan*, p. 702.

84. Quoted in Cannon, *President Reagan*, p. 702.

85. Schieffer and Gates, *The Acting President*, p. 292.

86. Quoted in Cannon, *President Reagan*, p. 712.

87. Quoted in Schieffer and Gates, *The Acting President*, p. 302.

88. Quoted in Cannon, *President Reagan*, p. 653.

89. Quoted in Mayer and McManus, *Landslide*, p. 389.

90. Quoted in Pemberton, *Exit with Honor*, p. 173.

91. Quoted in Strober and Strober, *Reagan*, p. 494.

92. Quoted in Strober and Strober, *Reagan*, p. 494.

93. Quoted in Cannon, *President Reagan*, p. 589.

Chapter Seven: Reagan's Legacy

94. Quoted in Cannon, *President Reagan*, p. 18.

95. Quoted in Cannon, *President Reagan*, p. 741.

96. Quoted in Cannon, *President Reagan*, p. 741.

97. Reagan, *An American Life*, p. 683.

98. Martin Anderson, *Revolution: The Reagan Legacy*. Stanford, CA: Hoover Institute Press, 1990, p. 434.

99. Pemberton, *Exit with Honor*, p. 97.

100. Quoted in Cannon, *President Reagan*, p. 826.

101. Quoted in Strober and Strober, *Reagan*, p. 136.

102. Quoted in Cannon, *President Reagan*, p. 793.

103. Quoted in Larry Berman, ed., *Looking Back on the Reagan Presidency*. Baltimore: Johns Hopkins University Press, 1990, p. 8.

104. Quoted in Schieffer and Gates, *The Acting President*, p. 378.

105. Reagan, *Speaking My Mind*, p. 417.

For Further Reading

J. H. Cardigan, *Ronald Reagan: A Remarkable Life.* Kansas City: Ariel Books, 1995. A look at Reagan's life, with a focus on his early years and movie career. Excellent photographs.

Zachary Kent, *Ronald Reagan.* Chicago: Children's Press, 1989. Biography of the fortieth president.

Don Lawson, *The Picture Life of Ronald Reagan.* New York: Franklin Watts, 1985. The story of Reagan's journey from boyhood in Illinois to the presidency.

Peter B. Levy, *Encyclopedia of the Reagan-Bush Years.* Westport, CT: Greenwood Press, 1996. Alphabetical listing of the key people, places, and events of the Reagan and Bush presidencies.

Nancy Reagan, *My Turn: The Memoirs of Nancy Reagan.* New York: Random House, 1989. The controversial First Lady tells her version of events in the Reagan White House.

Renée Schwartzberg, *Ronald Reagan.* New York: Chelsea House Publishers, 1991. Overview of Reagan's life, written for children and young adults.

L. B. Taylor Jr., *The New Right.* New York: Franklin Watts, 1981. Traces the development and key figures of the New Right movement.

Works Consulted

Martin Anderson, *Revolution: The Reagan Legacy.* Stanford, CA: Hoover Institute Press, 1990. A former policy adviser looks back on the Reagan years.

Laurence I. Barrett, *Gambling with History: Reagan in the White House.* New York: Penguin Books, 1984. A look at Reagan's second term, as well as an examination of the circumstances that surrounded the Iran-contra affair.

Larry Berman, ed., *Looking Back on the Reagan Presidency.* Baltimore: Johns Hopkins University Press, 1990. Nineteen political experts assess Ronald Reagan's performance as president.

Lou Cannon, *President Reagan: The Role of a Lifetime.* New York: Simon and Schuster, 1991. A comprehensive biography of the president, written by a reporter who covered Reagan from his days as governor of California through his presidency.

Thomas Carothers, *In the Name of Democracy: U.S Policy Toward Latin America in the Reagan Years.* Berkeley: University of California Press, 1991. A study of U.S. policy toward Central America during the 1980s.

Dinesh D'Souza, *Ronald Reagan: How an Ordinary Man Became an Extraordinary Leader.* New York: Simon and Schuster, 1997. Provides analysis of Reagan's leadership style from a sympathetic point of view.

Robert Dallek, *Ronald Reagan, The Politics of Symbolism.* Cambridge, MA: Harvard University Press, 1984. Examines the reasons for Reagan's broad appeal to the American public.

William A. Degregorio, *The Complete Book of U.S. Presidents.* New York: Random House, 1997. Outlines the major accomplishments and biographical details for every U.S. president through Clinton.

D. Erik Felten, ed., *A Shining City: The Legacy of Ronald Reagan.* New York: Simon and Schuster, 1998. Fifty speeches that Reagan gave in the years following his presidency, along with tributes from associates.

Fred I. Greenstein, ed., *The Reagan Presidency: An Early Assessment.* Baltimore: John Hopkins University Press, 1983. An analysis of Reagan's successes and failures over his first term.

Mark Hertsgaard, *On Bended Knee: The Press and the Reagan Presidency.* New York: Farrar Straus Giroux, 1988. Examines the relationship between Reagan and the press.

David W. Houck and Amos Kiewe, *A Shining City on the Hill: Ronald Reagan's Economic Rhetoric, 1951–1989.* New York: Praeger, 1991. A study of Reagan's various economic policies, beginning with his time in California.

Haynes Johnson, *Sleepwalking Through History: America in the Reagan Years.* New York: W. W. Norton and Company, 1991. An examination of the effect Reagan and his policies had on American society in the 1980s.

Walter Karp, *Liberty Under Siege: American Politics, 1976–1988.* New York: Henry Holt and Company, 1988. Traces the course of American politics during the Carter and Reagan presidencies.

Peter B. Levy, *Encyclopedia of the Reagan-Bush Years.* Westport, CT: Greenwood Press, 1996. Alphabetical listing of the key people, places, and events of the Reagan and Bush presidencies.

Jane Mayer and Doyle McManus, *Landslide: The Unmaking of the President 1984–1988.* Boston: Houghton Mifflin Company, 1988. A detailed account of the Iran-contra affair and the disputes among his advisers that hurt Reagan's effectiveness in his second term.

Edwin Meese III, *With Reagan: The Inside Story.* Washington, D.C.: Regnery Gateway, 1992. The former attorney general and longtime political adviser to Reagan gives readers a behind-the-scenes look at the Reagan presidency.

Michael Mendelbaum and Strobe Talbott, *Reagan and Gorbachev: The Chances for a Breakthrough in U.S.-Soviet Relations.* New York: Vintage Books, 1987. An early look at the developing relationship between Reagan and Soviet leader Gorbachev, along with an assessment of arms control negotiations.

William Ker Muir Jr., *The Bully Pulpit: The Presidential Leadership of Ronald Reagan.* San Francisco: ICS Press, 1992. From the conservative point of view, a look at Reagan's philosophy of self-reliance and smaller government.

William E. Pemberton, *Exit with Honor: The Life and Presidency of Ronald Reagan.* Armonk, NY: M. E. Sharpe, 1997. A balanced account of Reagan's personal and professional lives.

Ronald Reagan, *An American Life: The Autobiography of Ronald Reagan.* New York: Simon and Schuster, 1990. In his postpresidential autobiography, he discusses his path to Washington as well as the events of his eight years in office.

Ronald Reagan, *Speaking My Mind.* New York: Simon and Schuster, 1989. Selected Reagan speeches, starting with a 1951 speech to the Kiwanis International Convention and ending with his 1989 farewell address to the nation.

Michael Schaller, *Reckoning with Reagan: America and Its President in the 1980s.* New York: Oxford University Press, 1992. Highlights the political highs and lows of the Reagan years.

Bob Schieffer and Gary Paul Gates, *The Acting President.* New York: Dutton, 1989. A behind-the-scenes look at decision-making in the Reagan White House.

David A. Stockman, *The Triumph of Politics: The Inside Story of the Reagan Revolution.* New York: Avon, 1987. Reagan's former budget director makes a case for why Reaganomics did not work.

Deborah H. Strober and Gerald S. Strober, *Reagan: The Man and His Presidency.* Boston: Houghton Mifflin Company, 1998. Collection of interviews with members of Reagan's staff on subjects ranging from the Iran-contra affair to the AIDS crisis.

Index

Picture Credits

Cover Photo: Corbis

Archive Photos, 17, 51 (left), 54

Associated Press, 55, 61

Courtesy Jimmy Carter Library, 51 (right)

Courtesy Ronald Reagan Library, 10, 16, 18, 24, 31, 37, 45, 60, 63, 68, 70, 82, 86, 90, 93

Lee Frey/Archive Photos, 42

Imapress/Archive Photos, 41

Library of Congress, 13, 28, 85

Reuters/Tim Aubrey/Archive Photos, 33

Reuters/Jonathan Bainbridge/Archive Photos, 78

Reuters/Mike Guastella/Archive Photos, 14

Arnold Sachs/CNP/Archive Photos, 75

About the Author

Darv Johnson has a degree in American Studies from the University of North Carolina at Chapel Hill, and has worked for environmental conservation organizations in Washington D.C. and Seattle. He lives in Brooklyn, New York, where he writes freelance articles for magazines and is pursuing a master's degree in journalism from Columbia University. His other book for Lucent is *The Amazon Rain Forest*.